FOR LOVE AND GLORY

HIGH FLIGHT

Oh, I have slipped the surly bonds of earth,
And danced the skies on laughter-silvered wings;
Sunward I've climbed and joined the tumbling mirth
Of sun-split clouds – and done a hundred things
You have not dreamed of – wheeled and soared and swung
High in the sunlit silence. Hov'ring there,
I've chased the shouting wind along and flung
My eager craft through footless halls of air.
Up, up the long delirious, burning blue
I've topped the wind-swept heights with easy grace,
Where never lark, or even eagle, flew;
And, while with silent, lifting mind I've trod
The high untrespassed sanctity of space,
Put out my hand, and touched the face of God.

JOHN GILLESPIE MAGEE, JR.

FOR LOVE AND GLORY

A PICTORIAL HISTORY OF CANADA'S AIR FORCES

BY J.A. FOSTER

FOREWORD BY

AIR COMMODORE LEONARD J. BIRCHALL, O.B.E., D.F.C., C.D.

M&S

McClelland & Stewart Inc.
The Canadian Publishers
481 University Avenue
Toronto, Canada
M4B 3G2

CANADIAN CATALOGUING IN PUBLICATION DATA

Foster, J.A.
        For Love and Glory

ISBN 0-7710-3246-3

1. Canada - Air Force - History - Pictorial works
I. Title

DESIGN: Brant Cowie/ArtPlus Limited

PRINTED AND BOUND IN CANADA

Acknowledgement and thanks to National Archives of Canada, the National Aviation Museum, the Canadian Forces Photographic Unit, the Michael Hartley collection, and the research provided by Peter W. Foster, without whose help this book could not have been completed.

AUTHOR'S NOTE:

ON A SUNNY AFTERNOON in the early fifties, *en route* from Honduras to Canada, I landed a Canadian-registered Norseman at Broward County airport, near Fort Lauderdale. While customs clearance and refuelling activities were under way an older gentleman appeared on the tarmac to examine my aircraft. "They're a good machine," he told me. I agreed. "Flown far?" he inquired absently.

"San Pedro Sula. It's in Honduras," I hastened to add, in case he was unfamiliar with Central American geography. He nodded, then as an afterthought and with a disarming smile, introduced himself.

"I'm Billy Bishop."

We shook hands and for an hour or more we talked of flying and aircraft—two pilots who shared a common interest, a young international itinerant and a living legend. One thing Bishop said stands as clear, stark, and crystalline in my memory as it did nearly forty years ago. I had asked him why he joined the Royal Flying Corps, why he had wanted to become a pilot. He replied without a moment's hesitation.

"Why, for love and glory!"

This book is dedicated
to the memory of the late and very brave
Air Marshal William Avery Bishop,
V.C., M.C., D.S.O. & bar, D.F.C.

Contents

Foreword

THE GENESIS OF AND MAJOR IMPETUS to Canadian aviation came as a result of World War I, when our airmen demonstrated a natural aptitude and ability in the art of flying. The records and achievements of the Canadians in the skies over Europe were unequalled. It was therefore only natural that following the war these newly acquired skills should be put to use back home. The opponents were no longer enemy aircraft but the severe Canadian climate in the vast uninhabited and uncharted land that is our nation. In time this new enemy, too, was vanquished by the Canadian Air Forces with the same skill, courage, and determination that had given them victory in Europe.

As a result of their efforts, military aviation has played an important part in the development of Canada. Our extreme weather conditions, difficult surface travel, and great land mass made it financially impossible in 1918 for private enterprise to undertake large-scale exploration and development beyond the narrow corridor of railways and dirt roads that girdled our nation in the south. The north remained unexplored, uncharted, unsettled, and unknown. The Canadian government assumed responsibility for opening the north, and vested the operations for its implementation in the military. Thus, between the two world wars, a major portion of Canadian aviation activities was carried out, first by the Canadian Air Force, and then after 1 April, 1924, by the Royal Canadian Air Force.

For those who served in Canada's Air Forces this book will hold many memories. To former air crews, just seeing the types of aircraft they knew and flew will bring back all the details of harrowing experiences in war and peace. They will once more relive their courage and heroic deeds as faces of comrades no longer here pass in their mind's eye: a cramped and lonely fighter cockpit at dizzy heights, on constant alert for enemy attack; the long, tense haul of a bombing mission in dreary mind-numbing cold through cloud and storm, and constant battles with the enemy's day and night fighters culminating with the nerve-shattering run-in to the target through a heavy barrage of flak.

One aspect of Air Force history that cannot be stressed enough through pictures is the part played by the ground crews. They formed the overwhelming majority of our Air Forces. It was their skill, dependability and total commitment that made it possible for the air crews to carry out their missions. Nothing was possible without them. They were the ones who stood and watched *their* aircraft takeoff and disappear into the distance as they prayed silently for a safe return. They were the ones who waited on the tarmac for *their* aircraft to return; even when all hope had gone they kept *their* quiet, sad vigil in the belief that by some slim chance *their* aircraft would make it home. In the words of what has become known as the Anthem of the Erks… "Bless 'em all!"

As I look back over my more than fifty-five years of military service, I believe that the one thing above all else that has made it such a fascinating and rewarding life is the comradeship within the services. On the eve of World War II there were only 290 officers and 2,700 other ranks in the permanent RCAF. There were so few of us that we knew one another either personally or by reputation. This accounted for the great interest we shared in everyone's achievements, promotions, and adventures; and we were all affected by the same sadness from losses due to accidents. Despite the Air Force's rapid expansion during the war years this intimacy persisted. I believe it was due in great part to the element in which we operated — the air. The air bound us together regardless of our religious beliefs, racial origins, or language.

This book is a pictorial review of that life of comradeship in Canada's Air Forces, which have played such a dynamic and crucial part in our heritage. These traditions and characteristics developed in the RCAF exist as strongly in the present Air Command, and I am certain they will continue to thrive and flourish. I have the greatest pride in having been one of its members, and in having contributed in my own small way to its heritage.

AIR COMMODORE LEONARD J. BIRCHALL,
O.B.E., D.F.C., C.D.

Original *Silver Dart* in flight. (DEP'T. OF NATIONAL DEFENCE)

CHAPTER ONE

The Beginning

CANADA'S CONTRIBUTION to the development of aviation has been enormous. With a small population scattered across one of the largest land masses on earth Canadians have shared a belief that the airplane is a necessity for the exploration, development, and defence of their country. In 1909, when other nations still looked upon flying machines as mere mechanical curiosities, the Aerial Experimental Association of Baddeck, Nova Scotia, chaired by Alexander Graham Bell and his wife, Mabel, produced the first manned flying machine to operate successfully within the British Empire: J.A.D. McCurdy's historic flight in *Silver Dart* on 23 February ushered Canada into the aviation era.

History credits the Wright brothers with the world's first manned flight. Their triumphant flight at Kitty Hawk, North Carolina, on 17 December, 1903, lasted fifty-nine seconds at an estimated speed of 30/mph. Two years later the Wrights had increased that time aloft to thirty-eight minutes over a twenty-four-mile circular course. Believing their machine to have reached a stage of practical usefulness, Wilbur Wright went to Europe in 1908 to sell French rights to a syndicate of aviation enthusiasts. His flights at Le Mans, Pau, and Rome attracted world-wide attention and were attended by the kings of England, Spain, and Italy. Honours were showered upon him.

Despite the cheering, the Wright aircraft had serious flaws. It was unstable, difficult to control in anything but the calmest air conditions, and relied on manual wing warping by the pilot for lateral control. The team of young engineers working with Alexander Graham Bell was well on its way to solving these problems. Ailerons, tricycle undercarriage, rudder, control surfaces, pontoons, and engine designs developed for the AEA by Canadians J.A.D. McCurdy and Casey Baldwin, and Americans Thomas Selfridge and Glenn Curtiss formed the basis for the Curtiss Aircraft Company, later the giant American Curtiss-Wright Corporation.

McCurdy and Baldwin, with financial backing from the Bells, organized the Canadian Aerodrome Company to manufacture aircraft at Bell's summer home near Baddeck. During the summer of 1909 they built and shipped three aircraft by train to Camp Petawawa. There, before a group of sceptical military officers and government officials, they attempted to prove the potential of their airplanes as military weapons. The results were less than spectacular. Although *Silver Dart* made five separate flights of 50/mph at fifty feet, McCurdy, blinded by the sun, clipped a sand dune on the fifth go around and demolished the fragile machine. The next day their second aircraft, *Baddeck No. 1*, crashed seventy yards after take-off.

Canadian military officials concluded that airplanes were amusing toys with no practical military value; they were better left to the private sector to develop. Discouraged, McCurdy and Baldwin returned to Baddeck, and Canadian aircraft development languished.

The British had realized the military possibilities of operating an air arm. On 13 May, 1912, the Royal Flying Corps was formed out of the Air Battalion of the Royal Engineers. The new RFC was divided into two wings: naval and military. The naval wing carried out flying training and experiments with seaplanes, airships, and land planes; the military wing concentrated on land-based planes. (Officers seconded from the two services into the RFC retained their army and naval ranks.) One Royal Navy sub-lieutenant complimented his army colleagues after a fifth fatal accident in as many days: "…in spite of accidents these army chaps do pull their weight and are great sports. We're all having a jolly good time learning the ropes."

Meanwhile, U.S. military contracts for developing the Wright and Curtiss machines were proceeding. Finally, an order from the U.S. Navy in 1912 for 150 Curtiss Model F flying boats equipped with the new Sperry gyroscopic autopilot placed America as the world leader in aviation. On both sides of the Atlantic, however, the "jolly good times" were ending.

CHAPTER TWO

World War I

THE FIRST TENTATIVE MOVES towards a Canadian air force began in 1914. Anxious not to be left behind in wartime the government quickly set up a provisional "Canadian Aviation Corps" consisting of two officers and an NCO — none of whom knew the first thing about flying — and a Burgess-Dunne biplane purchased from the United States. This portentous force was shipped to England, where one of the officers was killed on his first solo flight in a British trainer. The other returned home for re-muster into the cavalry. The Burgess-Dunne was never used and eventually was sold as scrap. Thereafter, young Canadians interested in aviation careers were encouraged to volunteer for the British flying services.

Canadian volunteers came from two sources. One was the front line fighting in France where soldiers, frustrated by the stalemate of war, were game for anything

Burgess-Dunne two-seater, Canada's first military aircraft, purchased in 1914. (DEP'T. OF NATIONAL DEFENCE, PL 115112)

that might take them from the misery of the trenches; the second volunteer group signed up in Canada. In late 1914 the Royal Flying Corps required applicants to hold a pilot's licence; few Canadians qualified. However, those who were turned down by the RFC were accepted into the newly formed Royal Naval Air Service on condition that they obtain a pilot's licence from a civilian flying school.

In 1915, the Curtiss School of Aviation was set up at Long Branch, on the outskirts of Toronto. The school's flying boats were based at Hanlan's Point on an island in the Toronto harbour. More than a thousand applicants arrived to start training on the school's six Curtiss JN-3 aircraft on wheels and in Curtiss Model F flying boats. Homer Smith and Arthur Ince became the school's first graduates. One by one the planes were damaged, repaired, damaged

again, repaired, wrecked, sunk, recovered, then finally written off and replaced.

Later that summer Curtiss Aeroplanes and Motors Limited, under the management of J.A.D. McCurdy, opened its doors in Toronto: the first aircraft-manufacturing factory in Canada.

Before the end of the year Canadian pilots in the RNAS were flying Sopwith Strutters at the Western Front. The Strutter, a flimsy two-seater biplane, had been used for bombing missions. It was unstable and tended to shed its wings in moderate turbulence. Any steep turn could tighten into a spin without warning. "A man has to be a hell of a pilot or a hell of a fool to fly one

Air Marshal L.S. Bredner, Wright Brothers School, Dayton, Ohio, 28 January 1915. His instructor was Jack Simpson. (DEP'T. OF NATIONAL DEFENCE, PL 14590)

and survive," Lieutenant Arthur Ince observed acidly after his first combat sortie. Nevertheless, on 14 December, 1915, flying solo, Ince shot down a German seaplane off the Belgian coast. His exploit marked the first Canadian aerial combat victory, for which he received the first aviation decoration — a Distinguished Service Cross.

Life expectancy for new pilots at the Front was three to six weeks. Inexperienced lads, some with less than twenty-five hours of flying time, were sent into the sky against veteran German fliers who routinely outmanoeuvred and outshot them with devastating results. René Fonck, the French scoring ace, discovered early in 1918 that at age twenty-four he was the oldest pilot in his squadron.

Initially, the Germans held a technical edge in the battle for the sky. Early in the war, Anthony Fokker, a brilliant young Dutch aircraft builder, had designed a timing gear that allowed the German guns to shoot through the aircraft propeller, something the British and French had been working on for months. German planes mounted with twin machine-guns could pour out six times the fire-power of Allied aircraft. It was not until early in 1916, when a German pilot lost his way and ran out of fuel behind Allied lines, that the secret was discovered. Swiftly, the Allied air forces equipped their aircraft engines with Fokker's new interrupter gear, putting Allied machines on an equal mechanical footing with the enemy's for the first time.

Late in 1916 the RNAS replaced the heart-stopping Strutters with faster and more manoeuvrable Sopwith Pup and French Nieuport machines. These were used to protect Allied naval bases along the coasts of France and Belgium.

Gentleman Cadet W.A. Bishop at Royal Military College, Kingston. He was about to be kicked out for cheating when he resigned in 1914 and enlisted in the Army. Bishop was a bumbling young man who failed at everything he tried until he became a pilot. Ironically, after the war, the college took credit for his astonishing accomplishments and honoured him. (DEP'T. OF NATIONAL DEFENCE, RE 21098)

Gradually and painfully Canadian pilots learned from their mistakes and from the few veterans who survived this new war in the air.

Flight Lieutenant Edward Grange became Canada's first flying "ace" in January 1917, when, during a four-day period, his guns brought down five German aircraft. Wounded in his last battle, he was awarded the DSC but saw no further action. By spring of that year the RFC was desperately short of aircraft and pilots. A decision was made to transfer the RNAS to bolster the thinning numbers of RFC men and machines along the Western Front. During "Bloody April" 1917 the RFC lost forty per cent of its air crew to

The First Canadian JN-4 Jenny. The most widely used trainer of World War I. About 3,000 of these machines were built in Canada between 1917 and 1918 by the Canadian Aeroplanes Company in Toronto. Of these, 680 were sent to the United States. The JN4 continued to be used until 1923. Capt. Brian Peck delivered Canada's first air mail in a Jenny. A gentle aircraft, with a top speed of 95/mph and a cruising speed of 65/mph, it was not a machine to operate in head winds.

(DEP'T. OF NATIONAL DEFENCE, RE 19143-1)

German guns despite its superiority in numbers.

Most famous among the Canadian RNAS pilots was Raymond Collishaw, who commanded a flight in 10 Squadron.

Right: Royal Aircraft Factory F.E. 2d aircraft A1 of the Royal Flying Corps, England, ca. 1916. (NATIONAL ARCHIVES OF CANADA PA123968)

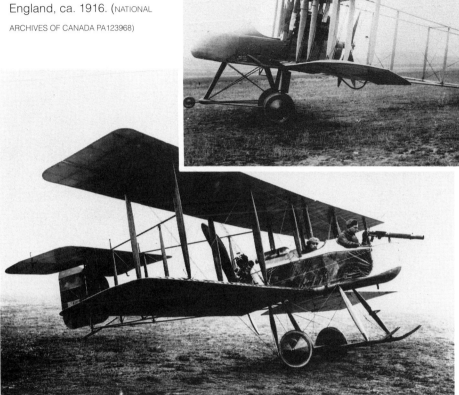

Vickers Gun Bus. (DEP'T. OF NATIONAL DEFENCE, AN 177)

Between May and July 1917 Collishaw's group of five Canadians claimed eighty-seven victories — thirty-three of them by Collishaw.

The superior abilities of the experienced German pilots are best illustrated by RFC losses after the Battle of the Somme: 800 RFC aircraft destroyed with a loss of 252 pilots against German losses of 359 aircraft and 43 dead. Although the British government and senior military officers considered Canadian pilots to be "semi-trained" it was the Canadian pilots who produced the lion's share of victories in the air. By the end of the war Billy Bishop led with 72 kills, Ray Collishaw was third with 60, D.R. MacLaren had 54 and W.G. Barker had 53. The Canadians' superiority lay in Canadian training methods. While Canada spent $10,000 per pilot on preliminary training alone the British spent half this amount on an entire pilot-training program.

Bishop credited his success in the air to the time he spent on the ground and in the air practising his marksmanship. Like the German ace Oswald Boelke, Bishop believed that if he "…flew in close enough his opponent would fall down." He regarded a plane as a mere gun platform from which to strike the enemy. An average pilot with no particular artistic flair for flying, Bishop trained himself to become one of the most deadly gunners in the sky. Only Germany's Baron Manfred von Richtofen and France's René Fonck had higher scores.

Canadian pilots lived considerably better than the troops in the trenches. They played sports, staged variety shows, organized rowdy mess parties, and took in the night life of Paris and London whenever they could manage a three-day pass. Yet for all the parties and boisterous fun the strain of combat took its toll on those who survived the odds. Three weeks after he shot down Baron von Richtofen over the

Major A.D. Carter of 123 Squadron in a captured Fokker D.VII. (NATIONAL ARCHIVES OF CANADA, PA 6017)

Australian sector, Canadian Roy Brown was invalided out to England with bleeding ulcers and the lined, haggard face of an old man. He had spent fourteen months at the Front.

The British War Office had a strangely inflexible attitude towards parachutes. They were provided to artillery spotters who went aloft in observation balloons above the Front, but they were not issued to flying personnel. Pilots wearing parachutes might burden the British tax-payer unnecessarily by bailing out of a damaged aircraft instead of trying to nurse it back to base. In most aircraft the fuel tank was located under the pilot's seat; as much of the ammunition used was tracer

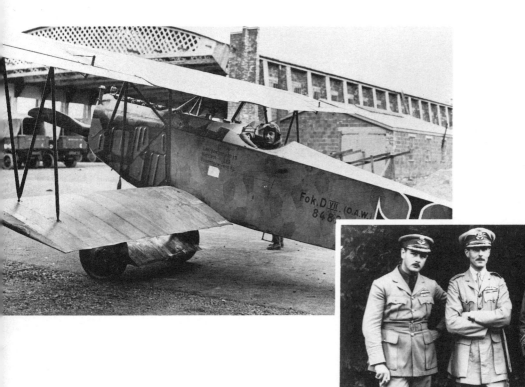

Right: Major W.G. Barker (right) with unidentified R.A.F. officers, Italy, c.1918. NATIONAL ARCHIVES OF CANADA C 59869

incendiary bullets, a pilot's greatest fear was spiralling helplessly to his death in a "flaming coffin." Edward Mannock, Britain's highest-scoring ace, carried a revolver on every flight to shoot himself should a direct hit turn his machine into a flamer. (German pilots wore parachutes because their High Command considered experienced flying personnel far more valuable than the aircraft.) Near the end of the war and due largely to the insistence of the Canadians the RFC permitted pilots to wear 'chutes.

By 1918 the wonder of the war was that pilots were able to fly at all. Much of the fighting took place at twenty thousand feet in open-cockpit airplanes with a wind chill factor of minus 70°. Bundled up pilots squeezed into their cockpits in sweltering summer temperatures at ground level, then climbed aloft to meet their enemy. They wore cellular cotton and silk underwear with several pullovers. Fur-lined boots and gauntlets over silk inners protected their hands and feet. Chamois-lined leather flying helmets were fitted over balaclavas to keep their heads and cheeks warm. Finally, whale oil was smeared over what remained exposed of their faces, which were then

L to R: Major A.D. Carter; Major Bailey; Captain W.B. Lawson, Officer Commanding, 123 Squadron; unknown. Upper Heywood, Oxford, England, May 1917. (NATIONAL ARCHIVES OF CANADA, PA 6020)

covered by fur-lined triplex goggles and a leather face mask. Once aloft, their warm breath iced their goggles continuously as aircraft propellers clawed for support in the thin air. It was anything but romantic.

Then it was over and those who survived sailed for home.

Work Shop of No. I Fighting Squadron, Canadian Air Force, Upper Heyford, Oxford, England, 1916.

(NATIONAL ARCHIVES OF CANADA, PA 6013)

Canadian Officers Royal Flying Corps, Reading, England, January 1916.

Front: J.W. Lockhart. First row (L to R) G.L. Main; W. Scatterty; C. Usborne; E.A. McKay; G.A. Lascelles; M.M. Sisley; F.S. Schell; J.P. Porter; G.S. Rogers; J.G. Ryrie; R.E. McBeth. Second row: W.E. McCoy; W.E. Soper; H.M. Fleming; H.C. Baker; H.M. Corbold; G. Thomson; E.D. Laurie; G.B. Ham; G.P. Alexander; L.M. McCoy; F.L. Hambly; J.R. Chamberlin; W.H. Hubbard; F.H. Stone

Third row: F.M. Carter; Wm. Carlyle; C.C. Campbell; W.E. Rowe; J.H. Ryan; J.S. Lee; N.D. Scott.

(NATIONAL ARCHIVES OF CANADA, C 26340)

A Canadian Royal Flying Corps JN4 crashes in Texas, winter 1917–1918. A good supply of wooden props was a must to keep the training scheme operational. (DEP'T. OF NATIONAL DEFENCE, PMR 73-803)

Sopwith Camel, port rear quarter view. Vintage aircraft at Rockcliffe. (DEP'T. OF NATIONAL DEFENCE, PL 140930)

On their way to the Front, soldiers on horseback
glance at a wrecked Sopwith Camel fighter.

(NATIONAL ARCHIVES OF CANADA, PA 3894)

Below: Canadian pilot Carl Falkenberg flew this Avro bomber on a daring raid against German zeppelin sheds in southern Germany.
(NATIONAL ARCHIVES OF CANADA, PA 6401)

Bottom: Training squadron of Curtiss JN-4s of the Royal Flying Corps Canada, at Camp Taliaferro, Fort Worth, Texas, 1917. (NATIONAL ARCHIVES OF CANADA, C 2494)

Handley-Page bomber of 100 Squadron. Second Lieutenants Charles H. Roy, pilot, and R. Roftus in the front gunner's position.

(DEP'T. OF NATIONAL DEFENCE, RE 69610)

This DH9 was flown by second Lieutenant John T. Rose of Toronto while he was with 224 Squadron in Italy late in 1918.

(DEP'T. OF NATIONAL DEFENCE, PMR 71355)

Above: French Nieuport.

(DEP'T. OF NATIONAL DEFENCE, PL 140914)

Below: A. Roy Brown and his Camel fighter at Birtangles, 209 Squadron. (DEP'T. OF NATIONAL DEFENCE, RE 18431-22)

Right: Billy Bishop—portrait taken during World War I. Credited with destroying seventy-two German planes Bishop was a shy, mild-mannered man on the ground and a careful and methodical killer in the air. He was awarded the Victoria Cross for attacking an enemy airfield alone during a dawn raid in which he destroyed three German aircraft.
(DEP'T. OF NATIONAL DEFENCE, RE 21089-1)

L to R Standing: unidentified; Perkins, Boldrick.
Seated: unidentified; Adjutant T. Watt; O. Turton; C. Creighton; W.L. Brintnell; unidentified. The background aircraft is a Curtiss JN4A. (NATIONAL ARCHIVES OF CANADA, PA 102814)

RFC officers of 42 Squadron, Bailleul, France, 1918. (DEP'T. OF NATIONAL DEFENCE, PMR 70045)

CHAPTER THREE

Between the Wars

AFTER THE WARTIME squadrons disbanded, Canada was left with little in the way of an air force. Politicians and idealists reasoned that with the formation of the League of Nations an enduring peace throughout the world was a foregone conclusion. There seemed little point to maintaining an air force.

In February 1919 the Overseas Club and Patriotic League in England sent Canada 16 aircraft and $170,000 worth of equipment in return for Canada's wartime service. This gift was followed by another from the United Kingdom of 101 planes, 12 dirigibles, 6 balloons, 19 dismantled hangars, and 300 motor vehicles. Like

other nations suffering under the delusion of permanent peace the British government could see no need to keep a combat-ready air force and the supporting infrastructure necessary to maintain it.

Never one to look a gift horse in the mouth, the Canadian government set up an Air Board to control military and civil aviation in the summer of 1919. After much discussion about what to do with the aviation equipment arriving from the United Kingdom, Parliament authorized the for-

Handley Page V/1500 aircraft "Atlantic", Harbour Grace, Nfld., ca. 10 June 1919.

(NATIONAL ARCHIVES OF CANADA, PA 121924)

'Tubby'   Kerr   Gran   Wyatt   Arnold   Clements.

The Crew starting for Canada   4 July 1919

Crew of Handley Page V/1500 aircraft "Atlantic" before flight from Harbour Grace, Nfld., to Parrsboro, N.S., 4 July 1919. (L to R) Major H.G. Brackley, Admiral Mark Kerr, Major Trygve Gran, Messrs. F. Wyatt, A.P. Arnold, C.C. Clements.

(NATIONAL ARCHIVES CANADA, PA 121927)

mation of a Canadian Air Force on 18 February, 1920. The 1,340 officers and 3,905 airmen comprising the new force were hired part-time. Following training, crews began flying in units formed to aid the provinces with forest-fire patrol, aerial survey, transport, and communications.

Early in 1922 it became obvious to those in government that aviation was far too important a service for its members to be part-time employees. Accordingly, on

THE DUMBELLS

I April, 1924, the Royal Canadian Air Force was created with a roster of full-time servicemen. The new RCAF continued in the area of civil aviation and instituted a training program. New aircraft were ordered from England in 1924, and the following year the Vickers Vedette, a Canadian version of the British Viking flying boat, was licensed for manufacture at the Vickers factory in Montreal. The move established the Canadian aircraft industry as a permanent part of the nation's growing industrial mosaic.

During the next few years the RCAF expanded quickly. The aircraft were mainly civilian designs. Avro 504Ks were replaced with 504N models. In 1927 the

The all-male Dumbells were Canada's most popular entertainment troupe during World War I, entertaining troops and airmen throughout the war zone with musical skits and comedy. After the war the Dumbells toured Canada for some time.

first of sixty-four DeHavilland DH 60 Moths were acquired along with a few Curtiss-Reid Ramblers. Some thirty-six Canadian-built Avro Avian Minor and Major trainers also entered service, as did several new Mk VI amphibian versions of the Vedette. In 1931 twenty Fleet Fawn I trainers, some Avro 621 Tutors, and several Fairchild 71 seaplanes were added to the hodgepodge of RCAF aircraft.

The military aspect of the air force although limited had not been entirely forgotten. A few Siskin III Fighters and Atlas Army Co-operation aircraft were purchased. However, the government's 1932 budget demonstrated where its priorities lay: $15 million for civil aviation; $2.5 million for the military branch. The Great Depression and resulting austerity measures undertaken by government slashed the air force to 103 officers and 591 airmen; as well, much of the civil air service was

abandoned and turned over to the commercial airlines and private-sector interests.

As tensions grew in Europe the RCAF began to regain strength. In 1935 the first of 24 Westland Wapiti bombers and seven Shark torpedo bombers were ordered. By 1937 five new air-force units and four Auxiliaries had been put into service. These Auxiliaries were intended to become bomber units, although Canada had no bombers at the time. The Department of Transport, formed the same year, finally freed the RCAF from all civil aviation.

Most promising of all, the new air-force budget was raised to $4.5 million. This encouraged a substantial aircraft-manufacturing industry and a purchase program for more modern aircraft was begun. In 1938 thirteen Westland Wapiti bombers were ordered from Britain; eighteen Supermarine Stranraer flying boats were also contracted. The Ottawa Car Manufacturing Company began building Wapiti bombers under licence, while Boeing Aircraft in Vancouver started work on a squadron of Blackburn Shark torpedo-bomber biplanes.

Handley Page V/1500 aircraft 'Atlantic' after crash landing at Parrsboro, N.S., 5 July 1919.

(NATIONAL ARCHIVES CANADA, PA 121937)

Every Hollywood dramatization about the perils of being a fighter pilot ignored the reality that airmen were dedicated killers.

In 1938 the aviation budget of $11 million rose to $30 million after the Munich Crisis. On 1 November the RCAF became an independent body responsible directly to the Minister of Defence. It was divided into three commands: Western Air, head-quartered in Vancouver; Eastern Air, head-quartered in Halifax; and Air Training, with headquarters in Toronto. The same year Britain asked Canada to manufacture Hawker Hurricanes, Handley-Page bombers, North American Harvards, Noorduyn Norsemen, and Westland Lysanders for the RAF.

By 1939, when Hitler invaded Poland, the RCAF had grown officially to 20 squadrons. The majority of these were either on paper or reserve units equipped with DeHavilland Tiger Moth trainers. The air-force roster comprised 4,061 officers and men with 270 aircraft. The RAF was rushing to equip 50 squadrons with men and 800 aircraft. (Field Marshal Göring's Luftwaffe had 124 fully equipped squadrons with more than 100,000 men and 3,800 aircraft.) On 10 September Canada declared war on Nazi Germany.

After Cadet C.S. Sheldon of Winnipeg stalled a JN-4 the plane crashed into a roof at Camp Borden, July 1919. (DEP'T. OF NATIONAL DEFENCE, PMR 71634)

Above: Handley-Page V1500 flight trials at
Cricklewood, 1 April, 1919.

(DEP'T. OF NATIONAL DEFENCE, PMR 73555)

Right: Bristol Fighter

(DEP'T OF NATIONAL DEFENCE, RE 13840)

Below: DeHavilland-4

(DEP'T OF NATIONAL DEFENCE, RE 1360)

Bottom: Camp Borden, 17 August, 1923.
The eight cadets of the first post-war pilot
training program: C.M. Anderson, E.J.
Durin, H.M. Durin, B.C. Glynn, R.E.
Knowles, C.R. Slemon, W.O. Stevens,
W.C. Weaver. (Slemon, second from left in
rear row, later became Air Marshal of the
RCAF.) (DEP'T OF NATIONAL DEFENCE, PL 117004)

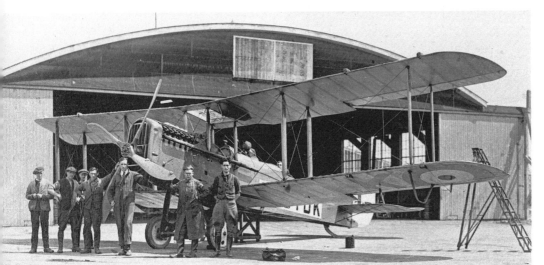

Avro Wright seaplane G-CYGK of
the RCAF, Shirley's Bay, Ont., 30
September 1925.

(NATIONAL ARCHIVES OF CANADA, PA 62416)

Sopwith Camel Exhibition Team
marching off the field at Camp
Borden after a demonstration of a
quick aircraft assembly.

(DEP'T. OF NATIONAL DEFENCE, PL 117006)

Avro 504K with generators installed on upper wing and strut for the new wireless equipment—which seldom worked.

(DEP'T. OF NATIONAL DEFENCE, PL 117001)

Aerial camera mounted on Avro 504N aircraft G-CYFY of the RCAF, Toronto, Ont., January 1925.

(NATIONAL ARCHIVES OF CANADA, PA 86993)

Propellor-swinging demonstration for new recruits,
Camp Borden, 1928. (DEP'T OF NATIONAL DEFENCE, PL 117009)

Model T Ford automatic starter on an Avro 504K—one of the very latest mechanical innovations of 1929. (DEP'T. OF NATIONAL DEFENCE, PMR 74568)

The Fairchild 24 R aircraft at Rockcliffe airport was used primarily for photographic mapping during the 1920s and 1930s.

(DEP'T OF NATIONAL DEFENCE, PL 1953)

Vickers Viking IV flying boat G-CYEZ of the RCAF, Manitoba, 19 August 1929.

(NATIONAL ARCHIVES OF CANADA C 27051)

Opposite: Canadian Vickers 'Vedette' II flying boat G-CYYF of the RCAF near Orient Bay, Ont., 1929-1930. (NATIONAL ARCHIVES OF CANADA, C 10450)

Above: Vickers Vigil training aircraft. Rockcliffe AFB, Ont., 19 August 1929.

(NATIONAL ARCHIVES OF CANADA, PA 062573)

Below: Avro Avian Mk IV Training aircraft with Genet Major engine, Rockcliffe AFB, Ont., 31 October 1929. (NATIONAL ARCHIVES OF CANADA, PA 062526)

Above: Ford Trimotor at St. Hubert, June 1931.

(DEP'T. OF NATIONAL DEFENCE, RE 16224)

Below: Artillery co-operation course, Camp Borden, 1931. Siskin message pick-up.

(DEP'T. OF NATIONAL DEFENCE, PMR 82183)

A damn cold proposition in winter! Ground crew hold down a Siskin revving to full speed for an engine check.

(DEP'T. OF NATIONAL DEFENCE, PL 117076)

Fleet (7C) Fawn.(DEP'T. OF
NATIONAL DEFENCE, RE 2308820)

Atlas (Armstrong-Whitworth)
27 July, 1935.
(DEP'T. OF NATIONAL DEFENCE, HC 7283)

Blackburn Shark, 7
November, 1936.
(DEP'T. OF NATIONAL DEFENCE, HC 7722)

Above: Supermarine Walrus, 6 November 1936. Designed by Reginald Mitchell, designer of the Spitfire, the lightly armed and slow Walrus was in operational use with the Royal Navy throughout the war from 1939 to the end on reconnaissance patrols and air-sea rescues. Eight machines served with the RCAF. Several pilots who crashed in the Great Lakes while training owe their lives to prompt pick-ups by the rugged-hulled Walrus.

(DEP'T. OF NATIONAL DEFENCE, HC 8126-2)

Left: Hawker Audax, 27 July, 1935.

(NATIONAL ARCHIVES OF CANADA, PA 063091)

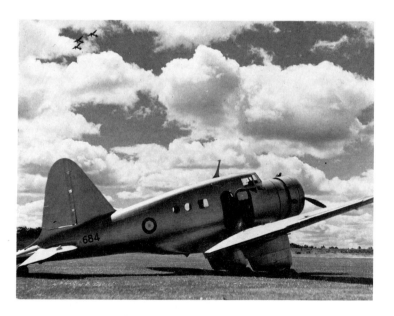

Northrop Delta. Twenty of these all-metal machines were built by Canadian Vickers and delivered to the RCAF in 1936. They were used for photography, maritime patrol, and as trainers.

(DEP'T. OF NATIONAL DEFENCE, PL 793)

Top left: Parachute packing at RCAF Station, Trenton, 1939. (DEP'T. OF NATIONAL DEFENCE, PMR 74275)

Top right: Officers rigging class, 111 Squadron, Vancouver, 15 January 1938.

(NATIONAL ARCHIVES OF CANADA, PA 133590)

Left: Noorduyn Norseman. The first of these splendid Canadian-built bush aircraft entered RCAF service in 1938. During the war 101 of these saw service across the country as light transports and wireless-school trainers with 6, 8, 119, 121, 166, and 167 squadrons. After the war they formed the backbone of RCAF search-and-rescue units. The Norseman carried eight passengers or 1,687 lbs. of cargo at a cruising speed of 150/mph. When production ceased in 1959, 923 Norsemen had been built.

(DEP'T. OF NATIONAL DEFENCE, PL 120871)

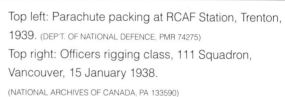

Fairchild Super 71D. (DEP'T. OF NATIONAL DEFENCE, RE 64973)

Airspeed Oxford aircraft no. 1503. Ottawa AFB, 6 June 1939. (NATIONAL ARCHIVES OF CANADA, PA 063384)

Inset: P/O John Gillespie Magee Jr. in his Spitfire, 412 "Falcon" Squadron. Wellingore, Lincolnshire, England, during the summer of 1941. Magee was killed in combat a few weeks later. His famous poem "High Flight" (see frontispiece), captures the experience of all pilots. (NATIONAL ARCHIVES OF CANADA, C-81431)

The Tiger Moth was the last in a long line of light biplanes built by DeHavilland in England and Canada. The Canadian production version had heated cockpits and a large sliding canopy. In all 1,384 Moths were used as elementary trainers by the RCAF beginning in 1937 and throughout the war at all Elementary Training Schools across the country. Powered by either a 145 hp Gipsy Major or 160 hp Menasco Pirate engine with a top speed of only 107/mph, the Moth was sturdy, simple to fly, and used extensively for aerobatic and instrument flying instruction. (DEP'T. OF NATIONAL DEFENCE, PL 3586)

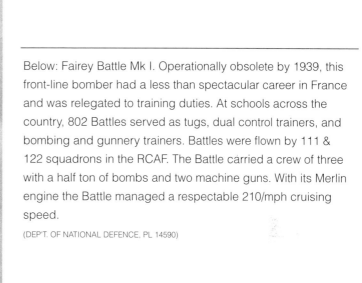

Below: Fairey Battle Mk I. Operationally obsolete by 1939, this front-line bomber had a less than spectacular career in France and was relegated to training duties. At schools across the country, 802 Battles served as tugs, dual control trainers, and bombing and gunnery trainers. Battles were flown by 111 & 122 squadrons in the RCAF. The Battle carried a crew of three with a half ton of bombs and two machine guns. With its Merlin engine the Battle managed a respectable 210/mph cruising speed.

(DEP'T. OF NATIONAL DEFENCE, PL 14590)

Westland Lysander of 110 Squadron, 8 January 1940. The first RCAF squadron to be sent overseas was equipped with Lysanders. Four "Lizze" squadrons operated in Canada for artillery spotting, target towing, reconnaissance, and close-support training. A Lysander shot down the first Heinkel bomber to fall in British Expeditionary Force territory in France. Equipped with long-range tanks, Lysanders were used to transport agents in and out of occupied territory. Top speed was 229/mph at 10,000 ft.

(DEP'T. OF NATIONAL DEFENCE, HC 9207)

Personnel awaiting kit inspection at summer camp of 111 Squadron, Sea Island, British Columbia, 9 June 1939.

(NATIONAL ARCHIVES OF CANADA, PA 133585)

CHAPTER FOUR

World War II

CANADA WAS QUICK off the mark in sending an air force to fight alongside the British. Two squadrons of the latest aircraft were sent by boat to England in 1940. However, the RCAF's main function was organizing the British Commonwealth Air Training Plan. Set up in 1939, it was designed to train air crews from all over the world. Canada's open spaces and good flying weather were a perfect setting. More than four thousand training aircraft were ordered, with instructors from the RCAF, RAF, and USAF. By the end of the war 131,533 air crew had passed through the ninety-seven training schools across the country. So effective was the BCATP that in early 1944 more than three thousand graduates per month were leaving the schools. The supply of trained personnel finally outstripped the overseas demand, and the training program had to be reduced.

While this massive training program was under way — new airports built, training aircraft constructed, shipped from England, or purchased from the United States — the

Boulton-Paul Defiant—a neat idea that didn't pan out. Designed as a surprise package against the standard enemy attack from the rear, the Defiant had no forward fire-power. When the Luftwaffe changed to head-on tactics the Defiants were relegated to target towing and training. A total of 1,060 Defiants were built between 1937 and 1943. RCAF 410 Squadron flew these machines from spring 1941 to summer 1942. (DEP'T. OF NATIONAL DEFENCE, PL 4641)

RCAF was divided into two forces: one protected Canadian shipping lanes from U-boat attacks in the North Atlantic and from Japanese forces in the Pacific; the other built a strong force to fight alongside the RAF overseas. Eventually the RCAF became the third largest air force among the Allied nations.

Consolidated Fleet Finch, 16B Mk II. Entered service with the RCAF in 1940 replacing the open-cockpit Fleet Fawn. A total of 661 Finches were flown as primary trainers at Elementary Training Schools across the country. Its 125 hp Kinner engine gave it a crusing speed of 98/mph and a range of 320 miles.

(DEP'T. OF NATIONAL DEFENCE, PL 1024)

Inset: Ox team pulling a Fleet Finch along a temporary taxiway at No. 17 Elementary Flying Training School, Stanley, Nova Scotia, 1941.

(DEP'T. OF NATIONAL DEFENCE, PMR 84977)

Grumman Goblin. Fifty-seven of these biplane fighters were built for export under licence by Canadian Car and Foundry. Fifteen of these went to the RCAF. The 118 Squadron at Rockcliffe, later moved to Dartmouth, was for a time the only force of fighters on Canada's east coast. Late in 1941 the Goblins were replaced by Curtiss Kittyhawks. The 123 (Army Co-operation) Squadron operated five Goblins for a time but had disposed of them by March 1942. Top speed was 216/mph. Armament consisted of three .30 Browning machine-guns: two in the observer's cockpit and one firing through the prop arc.

(DEP'T. OF NATIONAL DEFENCE, PL 5954)

RCAF kit layout, 1940. (NATIONAL ARCHIVES OF CANADA, PA 63769)

Members of the Women's Division receive, analyze, and plot information and movement of air, sea, and ground forces. Operational successes were dependent upon the accuracy and dedication of these women.

(DEP'T. OF NATIONAL DEFENCE, PL 14623)

Overseas Service

THE FIRST RCAF UNIT to reach England, in late February 1940, was 110 Squadron, equipped with Lysander IIs. It was followed by 1 Squadron in June. Its complement of Hurricanes was replaced with updated aircraft but the unit was not ready for action until August. The Canadians took to the air in time to join the Battle of Britain. To gain experience the unit operated initially under the wing of the RAF 111 Squadron. On 15 August, Squadron Leader E.A. McNabb shot down a Dornier 17 — the unit's first victory.

Bristol Beaufort. An RAF Coastal Command torpedo bomber used also for mine laying and reconnaissance. The 415 Squadron operated Beauforts for a brief period overseas. In Canada 149 Squadron flew Beauforts from Patricia Bay. It had four .303 cal. machine-guns and carried either a torpedo or 1,500 lbs. of bombs. Top speed at 6,000 ft. was 265/mph. (DEP'T. OF NATIONAL DEFENCE, PL 5395)

A few days later the squadron was declared operational and moved to Northolt Aerodrome; from there it began operations on 26 August. The new Hurricane pilots met with mixed fortunes in the weeks that followed: fourteen victories against twelve aircraft lost. Thereafter matters improved and by the time the unit was given its first break on 11 October, twenty-nine German aircraft had been shot down. The Allies lost fifteen Hurricanes and two pilots. There were seven wounded.

In late 1940, 112 Squadron reached England with no aircraft. Later, together with volunteers from 110 Squadron, they were supplied with Hurricanes and formed

RAF 242 Squadron in front of a Hurricane at Duxford, England, during the summer of 1940. (L to R) Denis Crowley-Milling; Hugh Tamblyn; Stan Turner; Saville (on wing); Neil Campbell; Willie McKnight; Douglas Bader (standing on his artificial legs); Eric Ball; Homer; Ben Brown. (NATIONAL ARCHIVES OF CANADA, C 61606)

into 2 Squadron RCAF based at Digby. To prevent confusion between the air-force units in Britain a reorganization was undertaken after 1940; numbers 400 to 449 were designated to the RCAF squadrons.

The first RCAF bomber squadron, 405, was formed in April 1941. Two reconnaissance units were organized shortly thereafter for Coastal Command using

Consolidated Catalina and giant Short Sunderland flying boats. Within eight months the RCAF in Britain grew from three to seventeen squadrons; five day fighters, three night fighters using Beaufighter IIs and Boulton Paul Defiants, two bombers, four with Coastal Command, and two Army Co-operation squadrons.

Above: Yale at No. 25 Flight Training School, Uplands Airport, December 1941.

(DEP'T. OF NATIONAL DEFENCE, RE 64-956)

Below: Cessna T-50 Crane twin-engine training aircraft no. 7658, Rockcliffe AFB, Ont., 12 September 1941. (NATIONAL ARCHIVES OF CANADA, PA 063986)

At Air Observation Schools under the British
Commonwealth Air Training Plan, more than 20,000
navigators, bombardiers, and wireless operators
trained on the Avro Anson during World War II. Nearly
three-quarters of the 4,395 machines produced were
built in Canada. The Anson had a crew of three and
was armed with three machine-guns and a 360-lb.
bomb load. It had a top speed of 180/mph at 7,000 ft.
The last Ansons were retired from the RCAF in 1954.

(DEP'T. OF NATIONAL DEFENCE, PL 9658)

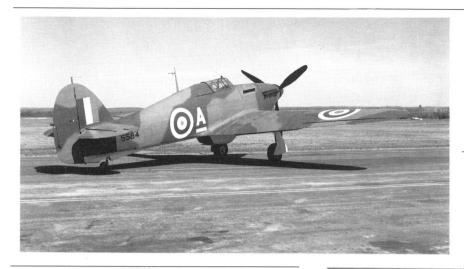

Below: FS Gunner H.W. Marfell in the turret of his Boulton Paul Defiant of 410 Squadron. (DEP'T. OF NATIONAL DEFENCE, PL 7436)

Above: Hawker Hurricane of 401 Squadron. First flown in 1935, the Hurricane served throughout World War II in every theatre of operations. The RCAF received its first Hurricanes in February 1939. First Canadian use of Hurricanes in combat was with 401 Squadron in the Battle of Britain. The 402 and 417 squadrons flew Hurricanes also. Ten Hurricane squadrons operated in Canada. A total of 1,451 of these machines were produced at the Canadian Car and Foundry Company in Fort William. While not as spectacular as the Spitfire it was a stronger and more reliable machine carrying 20mm and 40mm cannon, rockets, and up to one thousand lbs. of bombs. It had eight Browning machine-guns, a top speed of 360/mph at 17,500 ft., and a service ceiling of 36,000 ft.

(DEP'T. OF NATIONAL DEFENCE, PL 120920)

Left: Fleet Fort, 25 October 1941. Between 1941 and 1942, 101 of these oddly designed advanced trainers were delivered to the RCAF and used at Nos. 2 and 3 Wireless Schools in Calgary and Winnipeg until 1944. Using either a 250 hp or 330 hp Jacobs engine, the Fort had a top speed of 193/mph and a range of 610 miles.

(DEP'T. OF NATIONAL DEFENCE, HC 11763-4)

Supermarine Spitfire Mk II. The Hurricane and Spitfire were the main fighter aircraft throughout World War II. Although only eight were officially taken on strength by the RCAF, a number of Canadian squadrons flew Reginald Mitchell's wonderful fighter throughout the war. Many Canadian pilots flew them in RAF squadrons in other theatres. A powerful but gentle machine in the air, it had a tendency to ground loop — especially on pavement — during landing. The final Mk XIX version at war's end had a maximum speed of 460/mph.

(DEP'T. OF NATIONAL DEFENCE, PL 144710)

Bomber Command

By the end of 1941 four bomber squadrons were based in England: 419 was with 3 Group, 405 with 4 Group, and 408 and 420 were with 5 Group. Although small in comparison to its British cousins, the RCAF contingent was kept busy. Sixty-eight RCAF bombers took part in the thousand-plane raid on Cologne in May. The 405 Squadron became the first RCAF unit to change its twin-engined Vickers Wellingtons to new four-motored heavier Handley-Page Halifax IIs. Similar equipment reached the other squadrons during October.

A French-Canadian Squadron, 425, was formed in Yorkshire during June 1942 as part of 4 Group. It was joined later by 424 and 426 squadrons. The RCAF bomber force continued its expansion into late November when four more squadrons were organized and equipped with Wellingtons. This expansion preceded formation of a new all-Canadian 6 Bomber Group within RAF Air Marshal Harris's Bomber Command. It was a unique formation funded entirely by the Canadian government to "show the Canadian flag." Upon its inception on 1 January, 1943, seven RAF stations were handed over to the Canadians. By March this unit, known as 6 Group, had

The Lockheed Hudson IIIA bomber and ocean patrol aircraft joined the RCAF in the fall of 1939 and served until 1948. Top speed was 250/mph; 247 of these planes saw service in the RCAF on both coasts during World War II. (DEP'T. OF NATIONAL DEFENCE, PL 117989)

nine active squadrons.

Throughout the year, the RCAF bomber group constantly improved its aircraft, including new Canadian-built Avro Lancasters. Canada's contribution reached its peak early in 1944. After the summer of 1944, operations were conducted over Germany by day, as resistance from the Luftwaffe by then was much reduced. The biggest RCAF four-engine formation raid took place on 6 October when 293 Canadian Lancasters and Halifaxes raided Dortmund with a loss of only two aircraft. The RCAF Bomber Group suffered the smallest percentage loss of any Allied bomber commands.

A few days after the war ended, the squadrons began disbanding. Some were used to move liberated prisoners, three squadrons returned to Canada to aid in the war against Japan, and five units were used for transport purposes on the India Far East run. In August four more squadrons were given to the RAF Transport Command. By mid-May the few remaining units were disbanded.

Douglas Digby. Twenty of these DC-2 bomber versions operated on anti-submarine patrols off the east coast. (DEP'T. OF NATIONAL DEFENCE, PL 554)

Above: Bristol Bolingbroke Mk I, a Canadian-made version of the Bristol Blenheim, of which 626 served with the RCAF. Used for coastal patrol and anti-submarine work. A Bolingbroke from 115 Squadron was credited with sinking a Japanese submarine in 1942. (DEP'T. OF NATIONAL DEFENCE, PL 718)

Supermarine Stranraer flying boat of 6 Squadron, Alliford Bay, B.C., 10 November
1941. (NATIONAL ARCHIVES OF CANADA, PA 136890)

Fighter Command

AFTER ITS REST, refit, and training period 402 Squadron resumed operations with a sweep over France in April 1941. Most of the earlier Hurricane I models were replaced by Mk IIA versions during May. By August these were exchanged for the latest twelve-gun IIB models. The squadron spent its days in a series of long sweeps over the Channel. Equipped with new aircraft, 401 Squadron began operations on 23 July. It was joined later by 403 Squadron equipped with the spectacular new Spitfire Mk VB.

Eighteen months of cross-Channel sorties up and down the French and Belgian coasts provided nothing for the RCAF pilots to brag about. The older, experienced German pilots were more than a match for the green Canadians. Two and three fighter wings were dispatched in sorties and bomber escort raids in hopes of drawing up the Luftwaffe's thinning western air forces. It was at best an uneven contest, even when the Germans rose to the bait. The Messerschmitt BF 109F fighter was infinitely superior to the Hurricane and equal to the Spitfire Mk VB. Moreover, late in 1941, the new Focke-Wulf FW 190 appeared in the sky. It was superior to any-

Fairchild Mk II Cornell.

(DEP'T. OF NATIONAL DEFENCE, RE 19311-3)

Mosquito fuselage plywood shell halves being made on moulds. (BOEING CANADA DEHAVILLAND DIVISION)

thing in the Allied aviation arsenal. RAF and RCAF losses were embarrassingly high.

By the end of 1941 the Canadians had accomplished little; twenty-two confirmed victories for all five squadrons. New fighter squadrons were formed: 416 at Peterhead, 417 at Charmy Down. Six RCAF squadrons were operating during the first half of 1942. On 2 June the RCAF suffered its worst air defeat of the war when 403 Squadron was led off on a sweep of France with several RAF units. They were bounced by a swarm of German fighters. Seven Spitfires were shot down; one crash-landed. Only four returned to base.

In July 1942, 401 Squadron received new Spitfire Mk IXs. Then 402 Squadron was similarly equipped. During the Dieppe landings in August, Fighter Command provided the largest air cover ever mounted. The landings were a disaster and the air

Handley Page Hampden MkI AE 196 aircraft of 408 (Goose) Squadron, England, July 1941.

(NATIONAL ARCHIVES OF CANADA, PA 144774)

forces took their heaviest losses for a single day of the war: more than one hundred aircraft shot down.

As the Canadians grew accustomed to their new sleek Spitfire Mk IXs and discovered that they were at last on an equal footing with the FW 190s, their tactics changed from defensive to offensive. But 1942 brought little more success to the Canadians than 1941; only thirty-five victories for all seven squadrons combined and even heavier losses than in the previous year.

At the end of 1942 the Canadians were formed into two squadron RCAF wings within 11 Group. After Dieppe most RAF squadrons were moved to Africa, and the defence of Europe was left to the Commonwealth and foreign air forces. In early 1943 veteran RCAF pilots were returning for a second tour of duty. This pool of experienced fliers and the growing availability of Spitfire Mk IXs had remarkable results.

The U.S. heavy bomber offensive required Spitfire escorts until more USAF fighters could be put into the air. This increased activity forced the Luftwaffe to spread out its experienced fighter pilots and recruit new blood to replace its losses. Throughout 1943 fighting in the air seemed evenly matched, although gradually the Allies were gaining the upper hand. During April, RAF Wing Commander "Johnny" Johnson led the RCAF's Kenley Wing to its first of a string of spectacular victories. With only three losses during a month of operations Johnson's wing nailed seventeen German aircraft. May and June were equally successful. Johnson's tour ended when he led his men to a 4-0 victory over LeTouquent, Belgium. During this same period the Digby Wing also achieved some success over the North Sea.

The RCAF were able to claim 135 victo-ries in 1943. "Buck" McNair became the most successful Canadian pilot with a score of 13. RCAF fortunes were on the rise and they were about to rise even higher.

Above: Headquarters Staff, 6 Manning Depot, RCAF Women's Division, Toronto, 31 August, 1942.

(NATIONAL ARCHIVES OF CANADA, PA 125126)

Below: Personnel of the RCAF Women's Division arrive at St. John's, Newfoundland, 15 July 1942.

(NATIONAL ARCHIVES OF CANADA, PA 133895)

Airwomen mechanics at work in a Canadian
Women's Air Corps (CWAC) machine shop. 3 April
1942. (NATIONAL ARCHIVES OF CANADA, PA 108273)

Above: The DeHavilland fire department in action after a Mosquito crash. (BOEING CANADA DEHAVILLAND DIVISION)

Below: Radio Station of the Royal Canadian Air Force — Continuous Wave Unit Detachment No. 1 — main cabin under construction: Alliford Bay, B.C., 8 September 1942. (NATIONAL ARCHIVES OF CANADA, PA 141360)

DeHavilland women machinists working drill presses at Downsview, 1943. (BOEING CANADA DEHAVILLAND DIVISION)

Above: No. 2 Flying Training School at Uplands. Maintenance crews manage to keep the fleet of Harvard advanced trainers in the air despite sub-zero winter temperatures.

(DEP'T. OF NATIONAL DEFENCE, PL 14786)

Below: During September 1942 HRH Princess Alice, Air Commandant of the RCAF Women's Division, toured a variety of stations where members of the Women's Division were serving. W/C H.M. Kennedy, who piloted her aircraft, is pictured on the left. (DEP'T. OF NATIONAL DEFENCE, PL 11697)

Right: The Curtiss P-40 was probably the most widely used fighter of World War II and flown by more than a dozen air forces. Starting life as the Tomahawk, the Kittyhawk and Warhawk were improved versions of the same basic design. Four RCAF overseas squadrons beginning with 403 flew Tomahawks until February 1943. Six Canadian-based squadrons flew Kittyhawks; Squadrons 111 and 114 flew them in the Aleutian Islands campaign. Top speed was 345/mph with a normal range of 810 miles.(DEP'T. OF NATIONAL DEFENCE, PL 120883)

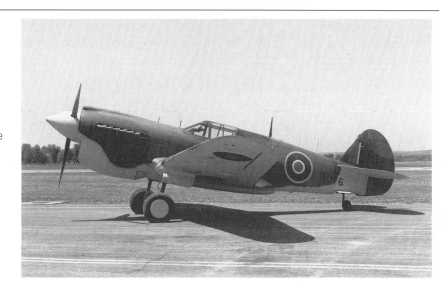

Below: Yales, Harvards, Ansons and Fairey Battles of the British Commonwealth Air Training Plan, Trenton, October 1942.

(DEP'T. OF NATIONAL DEFENCE, PMR 79279)

The Beurling family with
Prime Minister Mackenzie
King at the reception held for
them at the East Block of the
Parliament buildings, Ottawa.

(DEP'T. OF NATIONAL DEFENCE, PL 11971)

Wings presentation ceremony to the graduates of No. 2 SFTS, Uplands, by Prime Minister Mackenzie King on
Parliament Hill, 24 October, 1942. John Edgar MacDonald of San Marcos, Texas, is shown receiving his wings.

(DEP'T. OF NATIONAL DEFENCE, PL 11773)

Night Fighter Operations

THREE NIGHT-FIGHTER SQUADRONS were formed in 1941. All were based in the north of England, but with the Luftwaffe off fighting in Russia there were few alerts. A fourth unit, formed in Digby, became active in March of 1942. It flew Douglas Boston III intruder-bomber missions over France. Losses were heavy, and the four squadrons — 406, 409, 410, and 418 — brought down only fifteen aircraft in their first year of operations. Moreover, 1943 wasn't much better; only 410 Squadron armed with new DeHavilland Mosquitos chalked up eight victories over the North Sea. In April, 418 Squadron began replacing its Bostons with Mosquito VIs. The new planes gave pilots enough range to

Douglas Boston and Havoc 418 Squadron. The Boston and its fighter version, the Havoc, were used as night intruders. The 418 Squadron operated them until July 1943 when they were replaced by Mosquitos. Later models had an armament tray mounted in the belly with four 20mm cannon in addition to the aircraft's regular eight .303 machine-guns in the nose, dorsal, and ventral positions. Top speed was 303/mph. Gross weight was 25,000 lbs. (DEP'T. OF NATIONAL DEFENCE, PL 30963)

P/O Jimmy H. Whalen was a law student at the University of British Columbia when he enlisted. First posted to the Fleet Air Arm, "Smiling Jimmy" finally joined a Spitfire squadron in England, where he promptly bagged three ME 109s and sank a Flak Ship. Transferred to 30 (RAF) Squadron in Ceylon he shot down three Japanese 99 Navy bombers in August 1942.

(DEP'T. OF NATIONAL DEFENCE, PL 10028)

raid the Luftwaffe training schools in Denmark. By the end of August the squadron had nailed twenty German aircraft. In 1944, 418 Squadron downed 103 of the enemy, making it the most successful of the RCAF fighter units.

After receiving DeHavilland Mosquito XIIIs, 409 Squadron joined 410 Squadron to become part of the 2nd Tactical Air Force. The months that followed were moderately successful. Poor weather brought little action during September. The German retreat in Normandy permitted the squadrons to move across the channel later in the month to be based near Amiens, France. The German Ardennes operations during December brought an increase of air activity; by the end of the month the invasion scores were thirty-eight victories for 409 Squadron and forty-one for 410 Squadron against twelve losses.

During the summer, 418 Squadron was switched from intruder raids to intercepting pilotless V-1 "buzz-bombs" headed for London. They were relatively easy to catch and destroy. When encountering the bombs over water many pilots saved ammunition by lifting a wing of the V-1's wing with their own to send the bomb crashing into the sea. In all, sixty-eight of these flying bombs were brought down. After November the squadron was posted to 2 Group in the 2nd Tactical Air Force and thereafter concentrated on ground targets. Its intruder role was taken over by 400 Squadron, which achieved the same success as its sister squadron.

RCAF night fighter scores totalled 186 German aircraft in all — 50 for 406 Squadron, 62 for 409, and 74 for 410. The 418 Squadron claimed 102 victories in the air and 75 on the ground. The most successful Canadian night fighters were Russ

Staff Officers of the Women's Division confer in Ottawa, October 1942. L to R: F/O E.J.S. Henderson, No. 2 Training Command, Winnipeg; F/O Wila Walker, CO of the Women's Division Depot, Rockcliffe Station, Ottawa; Section Officer Silvia Evans, No. 4 Training Command, Calgary; F/O Marion Peiler, Eastern Command, Halifax; F/O Moira Drummond, No. 3 Training Command, Montreal; F/O Jean P. Davey, RCAF Medical Services; Squadron Officer K.O. Walker (head of table), Senior Officer of the Division; Section Officer M. Dunbar; Section Officer Jean T. Cameron, Western Air Command, Victoria; Section Officer M.M. Weekes of Air Force HQ; F/O W. Taylor, Women's Division, Manning Depot, Toronto; F/O E.M. Ward, Women's Division Depot, Rockcliffe; F/O Jean Cumming, No. 1 Training Command, Toronto.

(DEP'T. OF NATIONAL DEFENCE, PL 11603)

Bannock (9 in the air and two on the ground, plus 19 V-1s) and R.A. Kipp (credited with 2 on the ground and 10 $\frac{1}{2}$ in the air) — good shooting by any standard!

Riggers LAC J. Dewick and Cpl. E.L. Askew, members of an Overseas Army Co-op Squadron, check the landing gear on a Curtiss Tomahawk. Odiham, Hampshire, 22 April, 1942.

(DEP'T. OF NATIONAL DEFENCE, PL 7560)

Above: Consolidated Canso aircraft and personnel of 116 (BR) Squadron, Botwood, Newfoundland, October 1943. (NATIONAL ARCHIVES OF CANADA, PA 114775)

Below: Winter testing of Mosquitos at Downsview, 1944. (BOEING CANADA DEHAVILLAND DIVISION)

Reconnaissance Operations

BY LATE 1941 two Army Co-operation Squadrons had been formed and equipped with Curtiss Tomahawks. As these machines were unable to compete with regular front-line fighters the squadrons saw no real action until 1942, when both reconnaissance units were equipped with new North American P-51 Mustangs. The two-thousand-mile range Mustang with its considerable fire-power and speed proved to be the ideal reconnaissance aircraft of the war.

A partially formed reconnaissance unit took part in the Dieppe landings. Soon after, both 400 and 414 Squadrons were fully operational and flying regular intrud-er missions and shipping reconnaissance under such code names as LAGOON, INSTEP, and JIM CROW. On 1 January, 1943 a third reconnaissance squadron, 430, was formed with P-51 Mustangs. All

---

Hawker Typhoon. Three RCAF squadrons, 438, 439 and 440, served in 2nd Tactical Air Force and were part of the air assault that wrecked the German panzer divisions at Caen, Falaise, and North-West Europe. Armed with four 20mm cannon and carrying up to 2,000 lbs. of bombs at 405/mph, it was a formidable machine for low-level attacks. Unfortunately, its huge Napier engine made it dangerous for combat operations at high altitudes. (DEP'T. OF NATIONAL DEFENCE, PL 143334)

squadrons were transferred later in the year to Fighter Command. Cameras were attached to the planes, and regular weekly photo runs of the German coastal defences of Europe began.

The 2nd Tactical Air Force came into existence on 2 November, 1943, and all squadrons were transferred into this force. During the following months the units met with great success. The German Ardennes offensive brought a period of nearly continuous action for the reconnaissance squadrons, and in spite of some early Allied losses in the push forward the RCAF recce units were soon able to set up bases in Germany at captured Luftwaffe airfields to support the final days of the Allied advance. When hostilities ended, all units remained in Germany with the occupation forces until August 1945.

Mosquito assembly line at Downsview,Ontario, 1943. (BOEING CANADA DEHAVILLAND DIVISION)

Above: Vickers Wellington. The geodetic-constructed "Wimpy" was designed by Barnes Wallis, the man responsible for developing the skip bombs that burst the great Rhur dams. Eleven RCAF bomber squadrons operated Wellingtons during World War II from 1941 to 1944. Bomb load was 4,500 lbs. with a range of 1,400 miles at a cruising speed of 210/mph. Six .303 cal. guns were mounted between the tail, nose, and waist positions. The aircraft were used also for mine sweeping, sea patrols, air-sea rescues, transports, and glider tugs. Using Wellingtons equipped with powerful search leigh lights, 407 squadron sank four U-boats.

(DEP'T. OF NATIONAL DEFENCE, PL 5391)

Above: Two of DeHavilland's most successful aircraft in 1943: Mosquito bomber and Tiger Moth trainer. (BOEING CANADA DEHAVILLAND DIVISION)

Left: S/L R.B. Newton, CO of 411 Squadron. (DEP'T. OF NATIONAL DEFENCE, PL 7915)

Above: A group of Canadian fighter pilots of 401 Squadron. L to R: FS J. Whitham of Edmonton, FS H. MacDonald of Toronto, P/O H.J. Merritt of Smithville at the controls, P/O F. Newton of Vancouver and Sgt. C.S. de Nacrede of Calgary.

(DEP'T. OF NATIONAL DEFENCE, PL 7334)

Below: (L to R) Sgts. Jack Marvel, Ernie Cairn, Don Scowen, Robert Ward, Jim Orr, Hector Rubin, Harvey Kieswetter, and F/O John Moutray, DFM, beside their Wellington during operational training.

(DEP'T. OF NATIONAL DEFENCE, PL 10317)

Above: Spitfire Mk 14.

(DEP'T. OF NATIONAL DEFENCE, RE 20421-4)

Below: 405 Squadron — "Berlin or Bust" Wellington in northern England. (L to R) FS C.W. Higgins, pilot; Sgt. H. Wigley, pilot; Sgt. L. J. Nadeau, wireless air-gunner; Sgt. F.H.J. Farrell, navigator; Sgt. A. Smith, gunner; Sgt. I. Watters, 2nd Wireless Air Gunner. Each crewman wears a mascot emblem of his plane. (DEP'T. OF NATIONAL DEFENCE, PL 7374)

Wellington bomber crew members of 405 Squadron.

(DEP'T. OF NATIONAL DEFENCE, PL 7370)

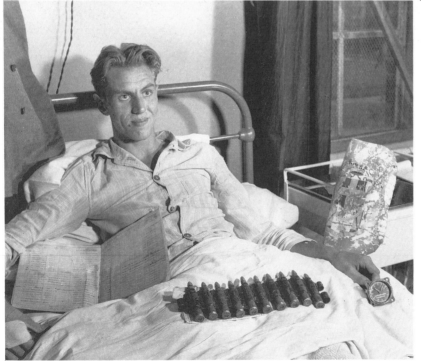

Above: Air Marshal Billy Bishop.

(DEP'T. OF NATIONAL DEFENCE, PL 10747)

Left: F/O George "Buzz" Beurling, DSO, DFC, DFM & Bar, the hero of Malta, recovering from injuries in an English hospital after the crash of a Liberator, in which he was a passenger, at Gibraltar.

(DEP'T. OF NATIONAL DEFENCE, PL 10976)

Members of the "W-Debs" entertainment group, who toured the RCAF stations in Bomber Group during 1943. L to R: LAW Lenor Barlow, Cpl. Cec Smith, Cpl. Audrey Canty, F/O Lola Davis, LAW Hazel Moore, LAW Winnie Kermath. (DEP'T. OF NATIONAL DEFENCE, PL 31180)

Avro Lancaster. A total of 7,378 of these bombers were built during World War II, 430 of them in Canada. Two Canadian Victoria Crosses were won by Lancaster crewmen Mynarksi and Bazelgette. Twelve RCAF squadrons operated Lancs. Easy to fly with a top speed of 270/mph the later versions could lift an incredible 23,000-lb. bomb load, 5,000 lbs. more than the much vaunted American B-17 Flying Fortress!

(DEP'T. OF NATIONAL DEFENCE, PL 44203)

Above: Mail plane Flying Fortress B-17, July 1944.

(NATIONAL ARCHIVES OF CANADA, PA 065072)

Above: Art Mitz, DFM, of Flint, Michigan, served with the RCAF in the Middle East. After a midair collision in January 1943, he bailed out over the desert and was listed officially as missing in action. A patrolling British tank crew picked him up and brought him back to his squadron.
(DEP'T. OF NATIONAL DEFENCE, PL 10235)

Below: Bristol Blenheim medium bomber was 40/mph faster than any fighter when it first appeared with the RAF in 1937. It went through a number of improvements during the war but was never a very popular aircraft with air crews. The Canadian Type 149 Bolingbroke was based on the Blenheim Mk I. The Blenheim was replaced by the DeHavilland Mosquito and Douglas Boston III bombers late in 1943. (DEP'T. OF NATIONAL DEFENCE, PL 4117)

Below: Firefighters attempt to remove a
Consolidated Liberator from a blazing No. 6
Hangar, Gander, Newfoundland, 4 June 1944.

(NATIONAL ARCHIVES OF CANADA, PA 145400)

Canso of 4 (BR) Squadron on patrol out of Ucluelet, Barkley Sound, B.C., 8 May, 1944.

(NATIONAL ARCHIVES OF CANADA, PA 136891)

The 2nd Tactical Air Force

THE FORMATION of the 2nd Tactical Air Force, in November 1943, divided fighters and fighter-bombers into two groups: one supporting the British 2nd Army, the other supporting the Canadian 1st Army. All but one of the RCAF Spitfire units were assigned to the 2nd TAC Air Force, and in the remaining weeks of 1943 they escorted U.S. and RAF bombers in attacking V-1 bases, Luftwaffe airfields, and German coastal defences.

Three new squadrons were formed in February 1944, each led by an experienced pilot and manned by veterans returning for their second and third tours of duty. In a short time these units contained the oldest, wisest, and best fighter pilots in the RCAF.

During the Normandy invasion on 6 June all three wings were heavily engaged. Fortunately, losses were light in spite of the tenacity shown by German defences throughout June and July. After the break-out from Caen and the destruction of the German 7th Army at Falaise, the Allied pursuit began. By September German forces had been driven back into their own country. In three summer months the nine Canadian squadrons claimed 262 victories.

A general German withdrawal reduced action in August and September, although Allied landings in Holland brought out

The "New Glasgow" Mosquito taking on bombs.

(BOEING CANADA DEHAVILLAND DIVISION)

91

what remained of the Luftwaffe. In early October the incredible Messerschmitt 262 jet fighter was encountered for the first time. Its 650/mph speed was a nasty shock to bomber and fighter crews alike. However, without adequate fuel, parts, and aircraft maintenance the Luftwaffe was a spent force. The Canadian squadrons began returning to England in rotation for modifications to carry thousand-pound bomb loads.

The Germans launched their beautifully timed Ardennes offensive in mid-December under cover of bad weather; Allied air forces remained grounded until Christmas. Thereafter, what remained of the Luftwaffe was engaged with ferocity until the Germans had little left to put into the sky. Throughout March and April the Allies concentrated on ground targets: one wing moved into Germany to support the rapidly advancing Allied armies. In the final days of the war Luftwaffe forces retreating from the Russian Front were engaged and brought down or intercepted while attempting escape to the Scandinavian countries.

The RCAF's wartime contribution to the 2nd Tactical Air Force was considerable: seven hundred victories in the air and on the ground. At war's end all units were based inside Germany; by March 1946 the last of these squadrons had disbanded.

Unloading casualties from France at Down Ampney, Gloucestershire, England, 8 August 1944.

(NATIONAL ARCHIVES OF CANADA, PA 128183)

Right: Four-thousand-pound bombs tumble from the bays of a Canadian Lancaster of 428 Squadron on the German garrison outside of LeHavre. The aiming point is enemy troop concentrations at the extreme right. This picture was taken by S/L Gerry Edwards flying in another Lancaster.

(DEP'T. OF NATIONAL DEFENCE, PL 32845)

Below: Members of 428 (Ghost) Squadron celebrate the unit's two thousandth bombing sortie with a specially decorated bomb for Bremen. Their Canadian-built Lancaster, *P-for-Peter*, carries the I.O.D.E. crest as a result of the squadron's adoption by the Toronto Chapter of that group.

(DEP'T. OF NATIONAL DEFENCE, PL 31970)

A 428 Squadron Halifax after completing its bombing run over LeHavre. Photo taken by F/L Frank Lynch who was flying a Lancaster on this mission. (DEP'T. OF NATIONAL DEFENCE, PL 32846)

Above: DeHavilland Mosquito Mk 25, DH98 A/A with feathered left engine.

(DEP'T. OF NATIONAL DEFENCE, PL 14571)

Below: WOs E.A. Ross and R.J. Legg watch an armourer affix a tail fin to a 500-lb. bomb for a Mitchell B-25. (DEP'T. OF NATIONAL DEFENCE, PL 31246)

Above: "Flame McGoon" of 418 Squadron, F/O S.N. May of Weston (left), and P/O J. Rich of Edmonton. (DEP'T. OF NATIONAL DEFENCE, PL 31294)

Right: Armourers of the RCAF 428 (Ghost) Squadron. (L to R) LACs Gord Robertson, Albert Packham, and George Roach.

(DEP'T. OF NATIONAL DEFENCE, PL 31170)

Above: Between German bombing raids engineers repair and extend the new runways at the Anzio Beachhead, June 1944.

(DEP'T. OF NATIONAL DEFENCE, PL 27517)

Below: Bristol Beaufighter. With a top speed of 320/mph, a 1,500-mile range, and fire-power from four cannon, six machine-guns, and either bombs or a torpedo, the Beaufighter was an ideal night fighter, coastal patrol, and anti-shipping bomber. It served in all theatres of war. The 404 Squadron operated Beaufighters from 1941 until the end of the war. (DEP'T. OF NATIONAL DEFENCE, PL 41049)

Lockheed Venturas of 149 (BR) Squadron, Terrace Bay, B.C., 26 June 1944. A military development from the civil transport Lockheed Lodestar, the Ventura served on both coasts for coastal patrol and anti-submarine duties, as a torpedo bomber, and for operational training. It had an 1,100-mile range, and a cruising speed of 300/mph with a crew of four. (NATIONAL ARCHIVES OF CANADA, PA 139554)

The Fairey Albacore was the last operational biplane used by the RCAF and the only one to see action. Designed to replace the Swordfish operating off RN carriers it served with distinction in several Mediterranean actions. A flight of 415 Squadron used Albacores after November 1943 for coastal operations. They operated alone and at night searching for enemy surface vessels. The machine cruised at 175/mph and carried a two-man crew and six 250-lb. bombs or one torpedo. (DEP'T. OF NATIONAL DEFENCE, PL 130494)

Coastal Command

RCAF INVOLVEMENT in Coastal Command covered all aspects of the war in the air, on land, and at sea: convoy patrol, coastal shipping surveillance, attacking German shipping in the North Sea, anti-submarine patrol, and air cover for commando raids along the French coast. The work was relentless and boring with only occasional moments of terror to break the monotony. Periodically Luftwaffe bombers and Condor flying boats were encountered and shot down during these patrols.

In the beginning RCAF Coastal Command overseas used Handley-Page Hampden twin-engine torpedo-bombers. In 1942 the Hampdens provided support to the RAF for some of the first thousand-aircraft bombing raids into Germany. As the war dragged on, Coastal Command units went on the offensive. In August a U-boat was damaged, and in September 1943 the squadrons converted to Bristol Beaufighter Mk Xs modified to carry rockets. With the arrival of new Vickers Wellington XIIIs and Fairey Albatross aircraft the squadrons began attacking German E boats at night. On one raid a German destroyer was set

The enemy surfaces to surrender to a coastal patrol aircraft. (DEP'T. OF NATIONAL DEFENCE, PL 44710)

99

ablaze.

A flying boat squadron using Consolidated Catalinas was formed in July 1941 for anti-shipping, anti-submarine, and regular patrol duties. It worked out of England, Scotland, the Shetland Islands, and Ceylon. A few of these aircraft were used to ship spare parts to the USSR, and to provide a transfer ferry service for air crews across the Atlantic. Later, the Catalinas were replaced with Short Sunderlands and used almost exclusively on escort and anti-submarine patrols. By late 1944 all but one of the RCAF's Coastal Command squadrons were engaged continuously on anti-sub duties. For a few months there was a sharp increase in German submarine activity as the enemy made a last desperate and futile stand.

RCAF Coastal Command 413 Squadron was the only unit actively involved in the war with Japan besides the eight thousand RCAF personnel who served in the Asian theatre of Burma and India with 435 and 436 squadrons. Leonard J. Birchall, of St.

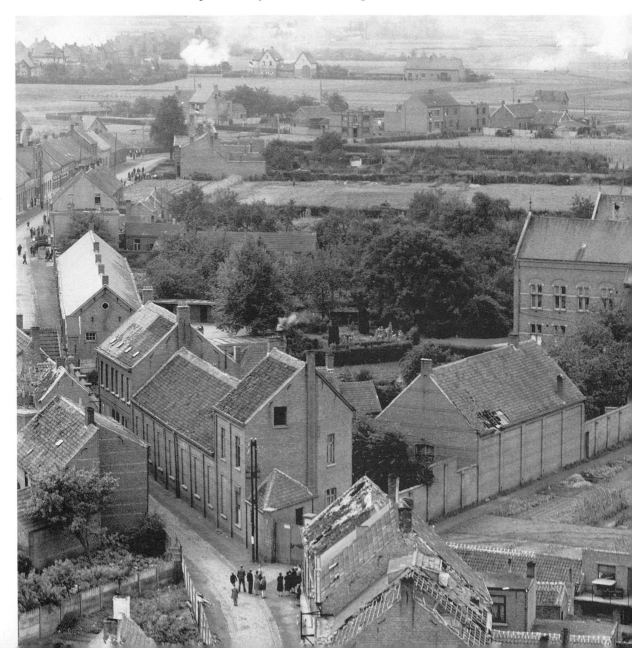

Catharines, Ontario, while flying a
Catalina patrol in the Indian Ocean, spotted
a Japanese Navy Task Force heading for
the island of Ceylon. He managed to radio
a warning to Allied Forces in the area
before he was shot down. His swift action
in the air resulted in the Japanese abandon-
ing their invasion of the island. He finished
the war in a Japanese concentration camp
and was later decorated as "The Saviour of
Ceylon." (Air Commodore Birchall, who
now resides in Kingston, Ontario, wrote
the introduction to this book.)

Top: Inspection by their Majesties and Princess
Elizabeth of an RCAF Bomber station in England,
11 August 1944. (DEP'T. OF NATIONAL DEFENCE, PL 31676)

Left: Orange smoke markers indicate to pilots
the Canadian troop positions. (DEP'T. OF NATIONAL
DEFENCE, PL 32692)

Below: German airmen who surrendered to officers at an RCAF airfield in Germany are
marched off under guard. (DEP'T. OF NATIONAL DEFENCE,
PL 44129)

WAAFs in mufti. Women of the RAF Gang Show at the first opening of the Malcolm Club in Normandy entertaining Canadian and British airmen. (DEP'T. OF NATIONAL DEFENCE, PL 31356)

Above: Recovery of Spitfire from 403 Squadron piloted by F/O Tosh of Almonte, Ontario, which was shot down by German flak and landed in a mine-field. (DEP'T. OF NATIONAL DEFENCE, PL 31130)

Inset: F/L R.J. Audet, DFC, of Calgary with his Spitfire. A member of 411 Squadron with several German air-craft to his credit Audet was killed in action on 3 March, 1945. (DEP'T. OF NATIONAL DEFENCE, PL 41718)

Below: Once the mines have been cleared an access road is built to reach the downed aircraft. (DEP'T. OF NATIONAL DEFENCE, PL 31127)

440 Squadron church service conducted by S/L Herbert E. Ashford, MBE, the wing padre.

(DEP'T. OF NATIONAL DEFENCE, PL 31431)

Other Theatres of War

MANY CANADIANS SERVED with the RAF in the Middle East from the start of the war. They were later joined by many RCAF personnel and served in Libya, Egypt, and in the defence of Malta. In the early months of the war, World War I veteran Ray Collishaw commanded the RAF in Egypt, and some of Canada's most famous pilots made their reputations in the Middle East.

Members of the RCNVR were among the early reinforcements sent to Burma.

One of these, Lieutenant Robert Hampton Gray, flying with the Royal Navy Fleet Air Arm, became the second Commonwealth pilot awarded a Victoria Cross, in recognition of his determined attack in Japan home waters against a Japanese frigate in one of the last raids of the war.

U-boat 625 being sunk by a Sunderland flying boat of 422 Squadron piloted by W/O 2 W.F. Morton and F/L S.W. Butler pilots, 10 March 1944.

(DEP'T. OF NATIONAL DEFENCE, RE 68586)

Inset: Wing Commander J.E. Fauquier, CO of 405 Squadron, with Butch, the unit's mascot, at Gransden Lodge.

(DEP'T. OF NATIONAL DEFENCE,PL 7352)

Pilots, airfield, and senior wing officers of the City of Ottawa (Beaver) 440 Squadron at one of the RCAF's advanced airfields in Normandy. The squadron's Alsatian mascot "Smoky" shares the limelight, July 1944.

(DEP'T. OF NATIONAL DEFENCE, PL 31057)

Top: Ansons mating, Vulcan, Alberta, 23 February 1944. No part of any training exercise.

(DEP'T. OF NATIONAL DEFENCE, RE 23061-11)

Bottom: The Consolidated Liberator had a 15.3 hour endurance at 165 mph with a crew of seven or eight. It carried 2,500 lbs. of depth charges, making it an ideal coastal-patrol aircraft or long-range bomber. Many were flown by Canadians in the RAF. One of these, F/O K.O. Moore, of 224 Squadron, sank two U-boats in twenty-two minutes, for which he won the DSO and American Silver Star. The 426 Squadron carried out 120 round trips between India and England with troops and supplies after VE Day before disbanding. In Canada, 149 Libs served with 10 (BR), 168 (Transport) and 5 (OTU Detachment) Squadrons.

(DEP'T. OF NATIONAL DEFENCE, RE 68-1276)

Members of 424 (Lancaster) Squadron. This photograph was taken shortly after VE-Day.

(DEP'T. OF NATIONAL DEFENCE, PL 44208)

Typhoon pilots of 440 Squadron in
France chat with Air Marshal, the
Viscount Lord Hugh Trenchard, father of
the RAF (with cane); and Air-Vice
Marshal Harry Broadhurst (with hand on
machine-gun). S/L Tommy Brannagan of
Windsor commanded the squadron.

(DEP'T. OF NATIONAL DEFENCE, PL 31059)

Above: S/L René Michaud of 409 Squadron places flowers on the grave of Mosquito pilot and friend, F/L "Long John" Peacock. Michaud is accompanied by the daughters of the French farmer whose land borders the cemetery.

(DEP'T. OF NATIONAL DEFENCE, PL 31923)

Right: Hostelbro, Denmark. Seven Canadian crew members from a bomber shot down over Jutland on 13 October, 1944, are re-interred from the field where they were buried by the Germans to the village's eight-hundred-year-old Lutheran cemetery. Five of the crew were identified: F/L R.D. Guild, F/O W.E. Jory, F/O V.L. Riley, F/O J.P. Grace, and F/O H.J. Loughran. (DEP'T. OF NATIONAL DEFENCE, PL 44871)

Above: VE-Day victory parade in the town of
Holborn. The Mayor, Wilfred E. Mullen, J.P., takes
the salute with Air Commodore E.E. Middelton,
CBE, from 1,200 RCAF officers, airmen, and airwomen as they swing past the town hall, 13 May
1945. (DEP'T. OF NATIONAL DEFENCE, PL 44053)

Opposite: Cpl. Frank Bastien of Trois Rivières
poses for the Danish Press with two Copenhagen
children during celebrations for the visit of Field
Marshal Bernard L. Montgomery.

(DEP'T. OF NATIONAL DEFENCE, PL 44059)

The wounded return home, 31 May, 1945.

(DEP'T. OF NATIONAL DEFENCE, PL 44176)

The RCAF Home Defence Force

IN 1937 CANADIAN CAR AND FOUNDRY were building Grumman Goblin aircraft for the Turkish Air Force. To bring the RCAF quickly to a wartime footing until new Canadian-built Hawker Hurricanes were available the government took fifteen Goblins. These were based at Saint John, New Brunswick, and eventually used for reconnaissance and patrol. The Goblins became the first fighter combat unit of the war. During the phony war, from September 1939 until May 1940, RCAF Eastern Command out of Dartmouth, Nova Scotia, patrolled the North Atlantic for submarines. Canadian-built Hawker Hurricanes first appeared in January 1940; but after the German invasion of France and the Low Countries, they were shipped to England to bolster Britain's island defences.

Imminent hostilities between Japan and the United States resulted in upgrading Western Air Command. Two new units were formed in August 1940, equipped with Bristol Bolingbrokes and Supermarine Stranraers, and an Army Co-operation unit was formed with Westland

First flown in 1943 the DeHavilland Vampire jet fighter was already obsolete when the first group of eighty-six machines entered RCAF service in 1946. Canada's first operational jet had a top speed of 548/mph and an incredibly flat gliding angle. The "Vamp" was a pilot's dream machine to fly. The last Vampire was retired from auxiliary squadrons in 1958. (DEP'T. OF NATIONAL DEFENCE, PC 253)

Lysanders and North American Harvards; however, Canada still had no fighting air force. The RAF was persuaded to relinquish seventy-two Curtiss Kittyhawk IA fighters and Lockheed Hudson IIIA bombers ordered from the United States; the new Hudsons were used on bomber reconnaissance duties.

North American P-51 Mustang. The finest long-range fighter of World War II. Early versions with American Allison engines lacked high-altitude performance and were used by the RAF for low-level reconnaissance and ground support. Its full potential was realized once the Allisons were replaced with Merlins. Five RCAF squadrons used Mustangs— 400, 414, 430, 441, and 442. After the war eighty-eight Mustang IVs were flown by regular and auxiliary squadrons until 1956. With the Merlin engine top speed was 440/mph. Armament was from four to eight .50 cal. guns.

(DEP'T. OF NATIONAL DEFENCE, PL 102919)

The Americans entered the war after the Japanese attacked Pearl Harbor. The war with Japan moved Canada closer to the fighting. New squadrons were transferred to Vancouver and Vancouver Island. A squadron of Kittyhawk fighters, two composite squadrons, and a ferry unit were organized. The west-coast crisis resulted in a nervous government ordering the formation of eight new fighter squadrons between April and July 1942. Hurricane Mk XI and XII versions due for overseas delivery were lifted from the production line and sent to equip the RCAF's new fighter squadrons for home defence.

Canada and the United States formed a close alliance for continental defence. During April 1942 a few RCAF Bolingbrokes were moved to Alaska and based at Annette Island and Yakutat to support the meagre U.S. forces defending the area. Western Air Command's first major

This Consolidated Liberator bomber was presented
to Canada by India.

(DEP'T. OF NATIONAL DEFENCE, RE 68-1276)

victory came on 7 July, 1942 when F/S
Thomas, on patrol in a Bolingbroke,
attacked the Japanese submarine RO32; his
bombs caused enough damage to prevent
the sub from diving. He then led U.S.
destroyers in to finish the job.

The United States was critically short of
pilots for its P-40 squadrons in the Pacific
throughout 1942. Canadians were sent to
fill the gap until American flying schools
could provide replacements. A new air
base was built on the island of Adak in the
Aleutians to enable the Americans to raid
the Japanese-held islands of Kiska and
Attu. The RCAF participated in some of
these early sorties, and on 26 September,
S/L K.A. Boomer shot down a Japanese
fighter float plane. This was the only aerial

victory for the RCAF home force during
the entire war, although a week later on the
east coast, F/L D.F. Raynes sank a German
U-boat.

Production of Consolidated Catalinas
and Cansos increased throughout 1943.
With America's vast manufacturing capaci-
ty geared for war, thousands of aircraft
were pouring off mass-production lines.
The RCAF acquired U.S. Consolidated
Liberators, Lockheed Ventura GRVs and
Lodestars, and Douglas Dakotas.
Production of Hurricanes ceased, and the
last group of these splendid old fighters
was sent to Russia. The RCAF home force
continued to grow with new squadrons and
new equipment.

The 13 Squadron received Spitfires and
Mitchell B-25s for reconnaissance. For
transport and specialty missions, 164 and
165 squadrons received Lodestars and
Dakotas. Heavy transport Boeing B-17
Fortresses and Consolidated Liberators

DHC 1 Chipmunk trainer. First test flight, 22 May, 1946.

(BOEING CANADA DEHAVILLAND DIVISION)

Auster Mk VI, 1948 to 1957.

(DEP'T. OF NATIONAL DEFENCE, RE 64-1863)

Above: North American Mitchell B-25. Many RCAF officers and men attached to RAF units operated Mitchells; they were used by 180 Squadron at Boundry Bay, B.C., for crews preparing to go to the Far East. After the war a quantity of Mitchells was supplied to RCAF auxiliary squadrons. The Mitchell was retired in 1962. At 292/mph top speed with a gross weight of 24,000 lbs., the B-25 was powered by two 1,350 hp Wright Cyclone engines.

(DEP'T. OF NATIONAL DEFENCE, PL 102640)

were sent to 168 Squadron. Numbers 5, 10, and 11 squadrons comprised the rest of the Home Force.

The Liberators enjoyed particular success against German U-boats on the East coast. On 19 September, 1943, F/L Fisher of 10 Squadron sank the U-341; on 26 October, F/L R.M. Aldwinkle—also from 10 Squadron—sank the U-420. By the end of the war Eastern Air Command's score would be six U-boats.

Japan had been placed on the defensive, and the Allies were busy planning an invasion of France. As the threat of attack faded, Canada's home forces began to shrink. In late 1943 six fighter squadrons were sent to Europe. By year's end the U-boat threat was finally contained. In March 1944 six units of the Home Force were disbanded and by October another six closed down operations.

Early in 1945 one of the two remaining home-fighter squadrons added a few DeHavilland Mosquito aircraft to its strength but by the time the Japanese surrendered, twelve more squadrons had disbanded. In May 1946 the RCAF was left with five squadrons.

Sikorski S-51. (DEP'T. OF NATIONAL DEFENCE, RE 66-638)

Douglas DC3 Dakota version Mk IV. The mainstay of Canadian, British, and American transport units throughout World War II, DC3s served in every combat theatre as troop transports, glider tugs, and ambulances. This machine was converted for VIP use. (DEP'T. OF NATIONAL DEFENCE, PL 102)

Comet - R.C.A.F aircraft DH106 with '412' trans-

port.   (BOEING CANADA DEHAVILLAND DIVISION)

The DeHavilland Chipmunk replaced the Harvard
as the air force basic trainer in the 1950s. It was
more economical to maintain and operate, and had
the advantage of using the large surplus of Gypsy
engines DeHavilland had on hand.

(BOEING CANADA DEHAVILLAND DIVISION)

CHAPTER FIVE

The Cold War Years

THE EARLY POST-WAR YEARS saw RCAF strength shrink to 12,000 men, six fighter squadrons equipped with new P-51D Mustangs, one squadron of Mitchell B-25s, and some Liberator B-24s. All Canadian armed forces were reunited under the Department of National Defence.

In 1947 Canadian armed forces were officially removed from wartime status and the building of a new RCAF began. The Liberators were replaced by Douglas DC3

Dakota transports. Two new squadrons were formed with Mustangs and Mitchells. DeHavilland Chipmunks were purchased for training purposes. Late in the year the RCAF took delivery of the first of its fleet of North Stars. These Canadair conversions of the Douglas DC-4 (the Douglas C-54 Skymaster in the USAF version) allowed surplus Rolls-Royce Merlin in-line engines to be used on the aircraft instead of American-made Pratt & Whitney radial motors. It made good economic sense, although the aircraft were noisy, especially in the passenger configuration adopted by Trans-Canada Airlines.

As tensions increased in Europe because of the Berlin Airlift of 1948 and the

Lockheed P2V-7 Neptune. Replaced the RCAF's Lancasters in 1955 for maritime patrol duties. Pod jet engines were added later bringing its top speed to more than 400/mph.

(DEP'T. OF NATIONAL DEFENCE, PL 95075)

USSR's general intractability, the Canadian government revised its defence policies. The ceiling on RCAF personnel was lifted and production of jet aircraft undertaken to counter a perceived threat from the Communist world. As a signatory in April 1949 to, the North Atlantic Treaty, Canada returned to its role of providing aviation training, now for other NATO members. In the splendid irony of peace, German and Italian former enemies became allies and friends. Canadair started production of T-33A jet trainers and the North American F-86 Sabre. Avro Canada joined with its English parent company, A.V. Roe, to produce the new Orenda all-jet engines for the Avro CF-100 "Canuck" fighter interceptor.

The war of words between Eastern and Western ideologies became one of weapons when in June 1950 North Korea invaded South Korea. Canadian aviation involvement was limited: one transport unit based in Washington flew regular service to Japan; and twenty Canadian pilots were attached to USAF units in Korea. Most were veterans of WWII, and their contribution to the Korean "police action" was impressive.

A new RCAF expansion program was announced in February 1951, due in part to the formation of the new Air Defence Command. Training began for 1 Air Division, Canada's NATO contribution. By September 1953, 1 Air Division was in Europe with its headquarters in the ancient Franco-German city of Metz. Equipped with three hundred aircraft, it formed a major part of NATO's air defence and was the best equipped of all air forces except the USAF's F-86F fighter wings.

Canada's home defence relied on the powerful new, all-weather Avro CF-100 interceptor. New weapons, radar, and fuel systems were developed for the CF-100. By 1954, fifty-five per cent of total defence spending was on the CF-100 program. Six new squadrons were formed, bringing Air Defence Command's total to nine. Unfortunately, the CF-100, like the Sopwith Strutter of WWI, had a nasty habit of shedding its wings if a pilot pulled a steady 6 Gs in a turn or pullout. Other RCAF squadrons received updated equipment, too: forty-eight Fairchild C-119F transports were ordered from the United States; one squadron received a pair of DeHavilland Comets and a Canadair C-5 for VIP duties.

During June 1953, Maritime and Tactical Commands were formed. The C-119 squadrons from Air Transport Command were assigned to TAC Command. It was discovered that the C-119 at operational gross weight could not maintain altitude in high temperatures on one engine. The RCAF had been had: ruefully, orders were given never to operate the aircraft at its designed gross.

To round out its search and rescue capabilities, which until now had been restricted to patrol aircraft and fast power boats, Air Transport Command received its first helicopters. Development of fighters continued throughout 1954 with the introduction of the Sabre Mk 5. The following year the CF-100s were upgraded. Finally, the RCAF reached its planned strength of forty-one squadrons with twenty-one types of aircraft, 2,968 in all. Regular RCAF personnel was composed of 49,500 men and women.

Sabre Mk 6s appeared in 1956 and were shipped to Europe to replace the Mk 5s. These new Sabres were superb machines, and for a year or more Canadians had the edge over all swept-wing aircraft in NATO forces.

When the United Nations arranged an

An RCAF North American Sabre Mk 6, sporting a NATO paint job. (DEP'T. OF NATIONAL DEFENCE, PL 108346)

international peace-keeping force in the Sinai Peninsula after the Suez crisis, Canada was asked to participate. Canadian troops were brought to the Middle East on RCAF North Stars. Logistical support was provided by the underpowered C-119s. Later, when the UN found itself involved in the chaos of the Congo after Belgium withdrew from its former colony, the RCAF's North Stars were again called into service.

At the end of 1957 the first Canadair Argus aircraft was delivered to the Air Force. Tactical fighters at home no longer appeared necessary, so the remaining P-51 Mustangs were declared obsolete. In place of fighters new transport squadrons were formed. A United States-Canada Defence Agreement was signed on 12 May, 1958. Nine Canadian squadrons were assigned to

Fairchild C-119 flying boxcar, the RCAF's principal Arctic supply and army transport aircraft for more than a decade, entered the service in 1952.

(DEP'T. OF NATIONAL DEFENCE, PL 124519)

Canadair CL 11 (C-5 RCAF designation). This aircraft was used to transport Princess Margaret on her 1958 Canadian tour.

(DEP'T. OF NATIONAL DEFENCE, PL 113370)

Opposite: Elevated BOMARC missile at RCAF Station North Bay, Ontario, 1957.

(NATIONAL ARCHIVES OF CANADA, PA 122740)

Above: Bristol Freighter. Six of these ungainly-looking machines were used by the RCAF from 1952 until 1967. They flew well and until the arrival of the Lockheed Hercules were the best freighters available at the time because of their clam-shell doors. British Air Ferries at Southend and Wardair bought the surplus aircraft from Crown Assets.

(DEP'T. OF NATIONAL DEFENCE, PL 63129)

North American Defence command (NORAD) headquartered in Colorado Springs. The NORAD command based its defence on three lines of radar stretching across northern Canada. They were called Pinetree, Mid-Canada, and DEW (Distant Early Warning). The last of these, the DEW line, was completed in 1958.

Throughout the 1950s Avro Canada had been working on a new supersonic interceptor, the CF-105 Arrow. First flown in March 1958, the Arrow proved to be the fastest and most sophisticated fighter aircraft in the world. But it was too big a project for Canada to undertake alone. The Americans refused to accept a Canadian aviation supplier for their defence requirements. By the end of the year the Canadian government decided inexplicably to scrap the entire program. All tooling, jigs, dies, and prototypes were to be destroyed. Experts at home and in England held the view that the future of air defence lay in guided missiles, not manned aircraft. It was a view that was to have serious repercussions both for the RCAF and RAF, and marked the end of major aircraft design and development in Canada.

Despite the belief in guided missiles the RCAF continued to grow. By the end of 1958 there were 56,000 men and women with more than 3,000 aircraft on the books, and newer aircraft were being ordered: Canadair CL-66 Cosmopolitans and Canadair Yukons.

The next year Lockheed F-104 Starfighters were chosen to replace the aging Sabres, and in 1960 Lockheed C-130 Hercules and DeHavilland DHC-5 Buffalo transports were ordered for the transport squadrons. That same year the government decided to abandon the BOMARC guided-missile program. This left the Air Force

with the problem of modernizing its aging fighter-aircraft equipment. A deal was worked out between Canada and the United States: the RCAF would acquire fifty-four two-seat McDonnell F-101 Voodoo fighters in exchange for Canadians taking over maintenance of the DEW line and contributing $10 million to the cost of building 150 Lockheed F-104 Starfighters for NATO forces.

The Voodoos joined the squadrons in 1961 and were followed in 1962 by delivery of the Starfighters in Canada and Europe. However, as the threat of attack from the Warsaw Pact nations appeared to recede, four of the RCAF squadrons in Europe and four from Canada's home defence force were disbanded. The last of the North Stars were also retired from service.

The government faced another of its endless financial crises in 1964. The defence budget was cut by $70 million, and three squadrons were disbanded in favour of guided missiles. The next year, still short of money, the RCAF's two utility squadrons were reduced to six aircraft and two helicopters; even the RCAF's "Golden Hawks" aerobatic team was dispersed. In Europe ten of the Starfighters had been lost in accidents. Keeping eight squadrons of eighteen aircraft in Europe without replacements presented the cost-conscious government with a problem: where to cut, yet still meet its NATO commitment. In the end, the force based at Cold Lake, Alberta, dropped from seventy to thirty aircraft; the forty surplus planes were shipped to Europe.

Later in 1964 a search began for a suitable machine to replace the Starfighter. RCAF experts considered the F-4 Phantom to be the best choice but were voted down

Avro CF-105 Arrow at St. Hubert, June 1958. The most advanced fighter plane in the world at the time. Only five were built. The project was scrapped as a government austerity measure and replaced with BOMARC missiles on the improbable theory that the day of manned fighters was over. Top speed was 1,650/mph with a gross weight of 76,000 lbs. (DEP'T. OF NATIONAL DEFENCE, PL 121044)

by the army and navy experts who felt it too sophisticated and expensive. Finally, early in 1965, the Northrop F-5A Freedom Fighter was chosen; from an initial wish list of 200 aircraft 115 were built. Canadian fighter aircraft were no longer in vogue; the government preferred investing its defence dollars in more practical Lockheed C-130 Hercules, new French Dassault Fan Jet Falcons, DeHavilland

The North American Harvard advanced trainer entered service in 1940. Built under licence by Canada Car and Foundry, the Harvard continued to serve as the air force trainer of choice until 1965. There were 2,258 built.

(DEP'T. OF NATIONAL DEFENCE, PL 132732)

Canadair version of the Lockheed T-33 trainer. It is still in use today after more than thirty-five years. Canadair built 656 of these reliable machines. Its top speed was 600/mph.

(DEP'T. OF NATIONAL DEFENCE, PL 99502)

DeHavilland Buffalo on the tarmac. (BOEING CANADA DEHAVILLAND DIVISION)

Right: Beech 18 Expeditor. From 1941 to 1968, 398 of these splendid seven-seater utility aircraft saw service in the RCAF. They were used for twin-engine, wireless, navigational training, VIP transport, and search and rescue. Engines were Pratt and Whitney 450 hp Wasps. Top speed was 210/mph when carrying its gross weight of 8,750 lb.
(DEP'T. OF NATIONAL DEFENCE, PL 132576)

McDonnell CF-101B Voodoo. The RCAF's front-line fighter of 1961. With a top speed of 1,220/mph, it was still no match for the Avro Arrow, which had been scrapped two years earlier through government stupidity. The last of the 132 Voodoos was retired in 1984. (DEP'T. OF NATIONAL DEFENCE, PL 150245)

Buffalos, and better engines for the aging fleet of Cosmopolitans.

Sadly, on 1 February, 1968, Canada's forces were unified as the Canadian Armed Forces, although some commands remained virtually intact: Maritime (now combined with the Naval Air Force), Mobile, Air Defence, and a combination of Transport and Training Command. The overseas European force remained under a separate command. The government felt that armed forces unification would cut costs. It didn't. Morale in all three services suffered, and many senior and experienced personnel resigned in disgust. The air force was little more than a third of the size it had been a decade earlier.

In June 1968, new Freedom Fighter aircraft began arriving; yet the old Starfighters were not replaced. Instead, two new squadrons were formed. At the same time fifty Bell CUH-IN helicopters were ordered. Then, in a sudden change of priorities, the government decided during the summer to reduce the country's air forces yet again. It came as a shock to NATO Command that Canada's reduced force was to become even smaller. All six CF-104 Starfighter squadrons in Europe were even-tually replaced with a smaller number of F-18s; NATO was informed that in the event of an emergency the machines could be flown back across the Atlantic.

Above: The Canadair-built Lockheed CF-104 entered service in 1961. Two hundred of these aircraft have provided the backbone of Canada's NATO commitment in Europe. Top speed is 1,450/mph. A pilot's dream to fly at cruising speed but lethal near the stall. The Luftwaffe nicknamed their fleet of 104s "widow-makers" after a series of fatal accidents.

(DEP'T. OF NATIONAL DEFENCE, PL 153016)

Right: Canadair 540 Cosmopolitan. A thirty-five-year air force veteran. Thirteen of these aircraft were delivered to the RCAF in 1960. A 360/mph turboprop conversion of the General Dynamics Convair.

(DEP'T. OF NATIONAL DEFENCE, PL 115324)

Top: A Sikorski H-34 of 100/8
Squadron, Rockcliffe, hovers
above the Ottawa River near the
airport.

(DEP'T. OF NATIONAL DEFENCE, PL 103742)

Right: DeHavilland T-64 Caribou.

(BOEING CANADA DEHAVILLAND DIVISION)

Right: Canadiar Yukon transport
of 437 Squadron over Niagara
Falls in November 1967. This turboprop transport was flown on
regular transatlantic flights
between Trenton, Ontario and
Marville, France.

(DEP'T. OF NATIONAL DEFENCE, PL 146235)

Above: An RCAF Piasecki H-21 Vertol helicopter lowers a fuel storage cell to a Mid-Canada Line radar site. The copter need not land to deliver a light load but can drop the cargo net once ground contact is made. (DEP'T. OF NATIONAL DEFENCE, PL 103688)

Below: Avro CF-100 Mk 4B of 445 Squadron.
(DEP'T. OF NATIONAL DEFENCE, RNC 33)

A trio of DeHavilland Twin Otters.

(BOEING CANADA DEHAVILLAND DIVISION)

Above: Bell, CH-118 Huey.

(DEP'T. OF NATIONAL DEFENCE, RE 711933)

Below: Canadair jet Tutor, an RCAF trainer now in use with top speed of 475/mph and 7,000 lbs. gross weight; 190 were built.

(DEP'T. OF NATIONAL DEFENCE, PL 99500)

CHAPTER SIX

The Years of Detente

LATE IN 1971 the government decided that two more squadrons should be scrapped. Detente between the United States and the USSR had come into vogue; there was no further need for air defence except to support the USAF, which would defend Canada in the event of war. Three squadrons of Voodoos remained to defend the entire Eastern Atlantic seaboard.

During the following years a few helicopter and transport purchases were made and a number of aging aircraft reconditioned. By the mid-1970s the only equipment that could be considered close to modern was the CF-5A Canadair version of the Freedom Fighters. Replacements were considered from time to time by the frugal government but in the end postponed indefinitely.

Finally, in 1979, when it became obvious that Canada's remaining fighter aircraft were incapable of fighting in modern combat conditions, the government agreed reluctantly to rearm the nation's skies. Various French and U.S. aircraft were examined. Ultimately a decision was made in 1980 to buy 137 McDonnell-Douglas F-18s. Early the following year Boeing 707s began replacing the Yukons, and in September of that same year the Aurora entered service with Maritime Command

Lockheed Hercules on a lapse drop, 17 February 1971. (DEP'T. OF NATIONAL DEFENCE, EN 71-70-1)

to replace the retiring Argus.

It may be that long-term government policy is right, that the time of global conflict is past, that air battles are obsolete. Yet the recorded history of civilization has repeatedly demonstrated that a strong country with a strong military presence seldom has anything to fear from a potential aggressor.

A Canadian Forces Tracker from VS-880 Squadron, CFB Shearwater, Nova Scotia, flies over the Canadian Coast Guard vessel *Chebucto*, March 1974, during a routine fishery surveillance off the Georges Bank.

(DEP'T. OF NATIONAL DEFENCE, IH 74-196)

Right: Boeing 707.

(DEP'T. OF NATIONAL DEFENCE, ISC 70-23-50)

Left: Canadair CI-600 Challenger, which serves on VIP duties with 412 Squadron at Ottawa. Top speed is 560/mph.

(DEP'T. OF NATIONAL DEFENCE, UPC 831558)

Below: Cockpit view of CF-18 fighters from 409 Tactical Fighter Squadron, CFB Baden-Söllingen, West Germany.

(DEP'T. OF NATIONAL DEFENCE, ISC 86-594)

Bottom: A CF-18 of 409 Tactical Squadron taxis from its hardened shelter at CFB Baden-Söllingen, West Germany.

(DEP'T. OF NATIONAL DEFENCE, ISC 86-608)

The motto of the Women's Branch during World War II was "We serve that men may fly." After years of arguments and dire predictions for and against allowing women to fly front-line fighters, the Armed forces accepted women in the same combat roles as men. The first two female fighter combat graduates were Captains Jane P. Foster (left) and Diana M. Brasseur (right), shown in front of a C5 Freedom Fighter after their training in 1988.

Index of Aircraft

Glossary of Ranks

AIR FORCE

ARMY